The Complete Guide To Attachment Styles

Learn to Navigate Anxious and Avoidant Patterns - How to Build Trust and Connection - Break Through Barriers to Vulverability - Tools and Techniques to Set Healthy Boundaries

Sage Lifestyle Press

SAGE LIFESTYLE
— PRESS —
EST. 2024

Contents

Introduction

People moved toward Jillian's calm and friendliness as soon as she entered a room. However, there was a pattern that had shaped every relationship she had ever known: a constant need for comfort, and a sensitivity to rejection that felt almost physical. Jillian thought these must be indicators of weakness or moral failings. What she didn't know was that they were the fingerprints of her attachment style, patterns acquired in her first relationships that today directed her interactions with others.

Like Jillian, each of us carries invisible blueprints for love and connection—stories written during our formative years. These tendencies define our reaction to intimacy, how we manage conflict, and how we guard against emotional injury. They affect whether we trust love when it shows up or wait for it to vanish, whether we reach for others during a crisis or withdraw into solitude.

Attachment theory provides a road map for these unconscious patterns. Developed over decades of research, it shows how our first interactions with caregivers form enduring models for all future relationships (Bowlby, 2021). Most importantly, though, it shows how these patterns can be grasped, questioned, and changed.

Things This Book Will Teach You

This book offers modern psychological research together with useful techniques for building better, more secure relationships. Every chapter develops the one before it, moving you from knowledge to real world application. Both linear reading and selective inquiry are intended uses for this book. If you are fresh to attachment theory, go from start to finish. If your style is known, start on the pertinent chapters. Research-based insights from eminent attachment researchers; practical exercises for instant use; real-life case studies highlighting important ideas; self-assessment tools for continuous development all throughout.

Keep a journal nearby. Writing about your experiences sharpens self-awareness and facilitates tracking of your development. Recall that healing attachment patterns is a slow process; be patient and gentle with yourself as you find fresh approaches to relating. Above all, approach this stuff with inquiry rather than criticism. Often, as creative responses to difficult situations, the patterns you will discover developed for good reasons. This book is about knowing what works and increasing your capacity for real, safe relationships; it is not about fixing what's broken.

Let's begin!

Free Bonus Content

Congratulations on taking an important step toward deeper self-understanding and healthier relationships.

As a thank you for reading *The Complete Guide to Attachment Styles*, I've created a special bonus to support you as you begin applying what you've learned.

Your **30-Day Self-Love Challenge** offers gentle daily prompts to help you build emotional safety and deepen your relationship with yourself.

Get Instant Access Now

Chapter One

Understanding Attachment Theory

E very culture has its love stories. Ancient Greek philosophers discussed the different types of love—eros, philia, and agape. Persian poets described love as a divine madness. Modern pop songs promise eternal devotion or lament its loss. All these varied expressions reveal a universal truth: humans naturally need connection. Attachment theory underscores this fundamental human need.

The need for love and connection isn't poetry or philosophy—it's biology, just like our need for sleep and rest.

Consider how love appears across time and place. Japanese concepts of 'koi' and 'ai' distinguish between passionate love and a deeper, nurturing connection. Dreamtime stories from Indigenous Australians convey profound connections between people, the land, and the spirit. African Ubuntu philosophy emphasizes that our humanity is deeply connected to our relationships with others. Diverse expressions of love and attachment point to something remarkable—a shared human understanding that transcends cultural boundaries.

The universal patterns are evident in everyday moments: a baby's smile, a child's hand reaching for their parent's, and couples' synced breathing. These aren't coincidences. They're expressions of our attachment system at work—a sophisticated neural network developed to ensure our survival through connection.

Research shows that secure relationships shape our brains, enhancing our capacity for emotional regulation, strengthening our immune systems, and increasing our resilience (Schwartz, 2014). When we experience consistent, nurturing connections, our bodies release oxytocin—the bonding hormone—creating biochemical rewards for staying close to those we love. This concept involves biology and behavior and creates patterns that influence every aspect of our lives.

Understanding attachment theory bridges these ancient wisdom traditions and modern science. It explains why the Greek philosophers and Persian poets described love so uniquely and why contemporary artists still struggle to capture its essence. Our capacity for attachment isn't just about survival—it's about thriving. It's about creating connections that give us the confidence to explore the world, knowing we have a secure base to return to.

This understanding opens new possibilities. Recognizing attachment as a biological imperative rather than a personal failing or success allows us to approach our relationships with greater compassion and clarity. Seeing our desire for connection not as neediness but as a fundamental aspect of being human provides a new perspective. We can learn to build stronger bonds by working with our attachment style rather than against it.

At its heart, attachment theory is a story of hope. It shows us that while our early experiences shape our expectations about relationships; they don't define our destiny. Our capacity for secure attachment can grow throughout our lives, nurtured by understanding and intention. This is where science meets possibility—in the space where knowledge transforms into wisdom, and wisdom leads to more fulfilling ways of connecting.

The Origins of the Attachment Theory

It all started with a simple question in the quiet halls of child psychology: Why do babies form such powerful bonds with their caregivers? No one knew the answer to this question would reshape our understanding of human connection for generations.

The mid-twentieth century held a straightforward belief about infant care; babies needed their mothers primarily for food and physical nurturing. However, Dr. John Bowlby (1907–1990) saw something different. Despite having their physical needs met, infants consistently displayed a strong desire for emotional connection. They sought more than sustenance; they craved safety, comfort, and understanding.

Bowlby was a British psychiatrist and psychoanalyst. His pioneering work has led many to consider him the founder of attachment theory. This theory is a significant part of psychology and focuses on the deep emotional bonds between people, especially between children and their primary caregivers.

Bowlby's revolutionary research started the field of attachment theory, which studies the strong connections people make with those who look after them. He argued children are biologically programmed to seek attachments as a survival mechanism. These early relationships significantly shape a child's emotional and social development. Bowlby identified secure attachment, which arises from consistent and nurturing care, as well as insecure attachment styles, which can result from neglect, inconsistency, or trauma. His research highlighted the critical role of a stable caregiver in fostering healthy psychological growth during childhood.

His observations sparked a scientific revolution in relationship psychology. Through meticulous research, he showed that our need for emotional bonds runs as deep as our need for food and shelter. These connections weren't optional extras—they were essential for survival, woven into human DNA through millions of years of evolution.

Mary Ainsworth, PhD (1913–1999) was a pioneering developmental psychologist best known for her work in attachment theory, building on the foundational ideas of Dr. Bowlby. Her contributions, particularly the development of the "Strange Situation" experiment, significantly expanded our understanding of how early relationships between children and caregivers shape emotional and social development. Ainsworth brought concrete evidence through her experiments. She documented how infants responded when their mothers left and returned to a room, revealing distinct patterns in how children seek and maintain a connection. These patterns reflected the deep and ongoing connection that had been developing between parent and child since birth.

Their combined research unveiled something profound: Our earliest relationships create templates that influence all future connections. Consistent care teaches children that the world is safe to explore, that others can be trusted, and that their emotions genuinely matter. These early lessons become blueprints for navigating relationships throughout life.

The implications stretched far beyond childhood. These fundamental patterns emerged everywhere: adult relationships, workplace dynamics, and how people cope with stress and seek support.

What began as observations of mothers and babies developed into a comprehensive framework for understanding human connection at every life stage. This new perspective significantly contributed to developmental psychology; rather than seeing dependency as a weakness to be overcome, research revealed it as a fundamental human need. When met with consistency and care, this need enables people to become more resilient, confident, and capable of meaningful connections.

These insights remain vital in our changing world. As new forms of connection and communication emerge, the core understanding holds: beneath our sophisticated adult relationships lie these basic patterns of human bonding, as essential today as when first observed decades ago.

Key Concepts

Human connections follow distinct patterns. Each pattern shapes how we approach love, trust, and emotional intimacy. Scientists call these patterns secure, anxious, avoidant, and disorganized. Each of these tells a different story about how people navigate relationships. The four primary attachment styles emerge from experiences.

The secure pattern represents balance. Secure people move through relationships naturally and are comfortable with closeness and independence. They express emotions clearly and maintain healthy boundaries. A secure person can share their deepest feelings while respecting their partner's need for space. They build trust naturally and recover well from conflict.

Most importantly, these patterns can change. While early experiences shape our relationship style, understanding creates room for growth. Through conscious effort and practice, people can develop more secure ways of connecting. This transformation begins with recognizing our pattern and understanding its origins.

In the following chapters, we'll explore each pattern in depth, examining its origins, manifestations, and paths toward growth. We'll uncover how these styles appear in daily life, from intimate relationships to professional settings, and provide practical tools for building stronger connections regardless of your starting point.

The Impact of Our Earliest Relationships

Long before we learn to speak, we learn to relate. Our brains create intricate connection patterns in life's first months and years. A mother's gentle touch, a father's consistent presence, and a caregiver's warm response to tears create the foundation for all future relationships.

Every interaction in our early childhood years teaches us something about connection. Do people come when we need them? Is it safe to trust? Will someone care about our feelings or dismiss them? These early lessons write into our nervous systems, creating patterns revealed decades later in ways we might not recognize.

Mary Main, PhD, a developmental psychologist at the University of California at Berkeley, pioneered research on adult attachment patterns in the 1980s. In 1985, she developed the Adult Attachment Interview, which revealed how early childhood experiences manifest in adult relationships. Consistent dismissal of a child's emotions may lead to an adult who struggles to identify their feelings. Someone who received unpredictable care might develop hypervigilance in relationships. Children naturally develop trust in relationships when they learn early on that their needs will be met.

These patterns reveal themselves in subtle ways. For instance, the executive who struggles to delegate might have learned early in their career that depending on others leads to disappointment. The partner who needs constant reassurance might have experienced unpredictable care in their earliest years. Friends who keep their distance might have learned too young that closeness brings pain.

Understanding these connections helps shift from judgment into compassion for ourselves and others walking similar paths.

The Attachment Theory in Modern Psychology

Therapists observe that relationship difficulties, work stress, and personal growth issues frequently arise from early attachment patterns. Patterns of attachment formed in childhood often influence adult behaviors, shaping how individuals navigate trust, intimacy, and independence in their relationships.

Consider some common patterns seen in counseling practices:

- **The Perfectionist**: Driven by a fear of disapproval, they strive to meet impossibly high standards to maintain acceptance.

- **The Caretaker**: Always offering support but rarely accepting it, they struggle to let others help them.

- **The High-Achiever**: Focused on success and maintaining emotional distance, they keep relationships at arm's length.

- **The People-Pleaser**: Eager to maintain harmony, they often lose their sense of self in relationships.

- **The Independent Spirit**: Fiercely self-reliant, they fear becoming "too needy" or dependent on others.

These patterns are not definitive labels, but are typical dynamics rooted in early attachment experiences. Understanding these tendencies can help individuals identify how their relational habits affect their well-being and explore healthier ways to connect with others.

This understanding of relationship patterns has revolutionized modern psychology. When someone steps into a therapist's office carrying the weight of trust issues or fear of abandonment, their healing often begins with exploring these fundamental patterns. It's like finding the source code of human connection—a key that unlocks a deeper understanding of why we love and relate the way we do.

Modern research continues to validate what therapists witness daily. For example, Dr. Dan Siegel's work on interpersonal neurobiology shows how early relationships literally shape our brain's architecture. Dr. Stephen Porges' polyvagal theory explains why our bodies respond to relationship stress in predictable patterns. Similarly, Dr. Sue Johnson's research through Emotionally Focused Therapy shows how these early blueprints influence our adult relationships.

Dr. Bessel van der Kolk, a leading figure in trauma research, explores how trauma and relationship patterns are stored in the body. His book *The Body Keeps the Score* is a cornerstone in understanding trauma's impact on the mind and body. Dr. Peter Levine developed Somatic Experiencing, a therapy approach that uses mindfulness and body awareness to heal trauma and reshape unhealthy patterns stored in the nervous system.

Even with insecure childhoods, secure attachment is consciously attainable, says trauma expert Dr. Diane Poole Heller. The research of Ainsworth and Main has laid this foundation, showing how attachment patterns pass through generations until someone chooses differently.

These framework paths, validated by decades of clinical research, lead to:

- Recognition of automatic responses to intimacy.

- Understanding of triggers and emotional patterns.

- Development of new communication styles.

- Creation of healthier boundaries.

- Building more secure relationships.

These findings offer hope. While early experiences shape us, they need not define us. Through conscious awareness and practice, we can develop new patterns of connection that better serve who we're becoming.

The beauty lies in our capacity for growth. While our past experiences may have created our first blueprint for connection, we're only bound to follow it for a while. With awareness comes choice, and with clarity comes the opportunity to write alternative stories. Attachment science explains our connection patterns and offers ways to create secure, authentic relationships.

Chapter Two

Identifying Your Attachment Style

D r. Sarah Chen sits across from her therapy client, Maya, who's describing her relationship patterns: "I fall hard and fast, then panic when they need space. My last three relationships ended the same way—me clinging tighter as they pulled away."

Meanwhile, across town, David explains to his friend: "I don't understand why she needs to talk about everything. When things get emotional, I just... shut down. It's like my brain goes offline."

Both Maya and David are describing attachment styles—consistent patterns in how we connect, respond to intimacy, and navigate relationship challenges (Bartholomew & Horowitz, 1991). These styles aren't personality traits or conscious choices; they're adaptive strategies developed in response to early caregiving experiences.

Subtle moments reveal attachment style: dinner interruptions, pauses, reactions to "We need to talk." These micro-moments, accumulated over years, create the unique fingerprint of how you love and connect.

The process of identification requires honest self-reflection, often revealing patterns we've been unconsciously repeating for decades. But this awareness becomes the foundation for conscious choice, transforming automatic reactions into intentional responses.

Understanding Attachment as Adaptation

Attachment styles represent our nervous system's learned responses to relationships (Porges, 2011). Each style developed as a solution to specific experiences:

- When caregiving was consistent and responsive, children learned relationships were safe (secure attachment)

- When care was unpredictable, children stayed alert to relationship threats (anxious attachment)

- When emotional needs were dismissed, children learned self-reliance (avoidant attachment)

- When caregivers were both comforting and frightening, children developed conflicted responses (disorganized attachment)

Understanding this removes judgment from attachment styles—each represents intelligent adaptation to early circumstances.

The Four Primary Styles

Secure Attachment (Approximately 50-60% of Adults)

Core Belief: "I am worthy of love, and others are trustworthy and available."

Relationship Approach: Comfortable with intimacy and autonomy, effective communication during conflict, ability to seek support and also to provide support appropriately.

Example: When Priya's partner mentions feeling stressed about work, she offers presence without trying to fix the problem. "That sounds really difficult. How can I best support you right now?" She can hold space for his emotions without taking them on as her own responsibility.

Childhood Origins: Consistent, responsive caregiving where emotional needs were acknowledged and met most of the time. Caregivers balanced support with encouragement of independence.

Anxious Attachment (Approximately 15-20% of Adults)

Core Belief: "I am worthy of love, but others might not be available or reliable."

Relationship Approach: Strong desire for closeness, sensitivity to partner's moods and availability, tendency to interpret neutral behaviors as relationship threats.

Example: When Marcus doesn't respond to texts for a few hours, Jessica's mind creates stories: "He's losing interest," "I said something wrong," "He's talking to someone else." These thoughts feel absolutely real, triggering physical anxiety and urges to reach out repeatedly.

Childhood Origins: Inconsistent caregiving where emotional needs were sometimes met enthusiastically and other times ignored or dismissed. This unpredictability created hypervigilance to relationship cues.

Avoidant Attachment (Approximately 20-25% of Adults)

Core Belief: "I must rely on myself because others may not be available or trustworthy."

Relationship Approach: Values independence, discomfort with emotional expression or vulnerability, tendency to minimize the importance of close relationships.

Example: When Kenji's girlfriend tries to discuss relationship issues, he feels overwhelmed and suggests "talking about it later." He genuinely cares, but finds emotional conversations suffocating. His instinct is to create space until the emotional intensity passes.

Childhood Origins: Caregiving that discouraged emotional expression or dependency. Children learned that needs were met more reliably when they didn't express them or appeared self-sufficient.

Disorganized Attachment (Approximately 5-10% of Adults)

Core Belief: "I want close relationships, but they feel dangerous and unpredictable."

Relationship Approach: Conflicting desires for intimacy and independence, difficulty regulating emotions in relationships, patterns of approach and avoidance that can seem contradictory.

Example: Aaliyah simultaneously craves closeness with her partner and feels terrified when he expresses love. She might plan their future together one day, then pick a fight and threaten to leave the next. Her nervous system can't decide if love means safety or danger.

Childhood Origins: Caregiving that was both a source of comfort and fear—often involving trauma, loss, or caregivers who were overwhelmed by their own emotional struggles.

Attachment Styles Across Cultures

Research shows attachment patterns exist across cultures, though expression varies (Van IJzendoorn & Sagi-Schwartz, 2008). For example:

Collectivist cultures may emphasize interdependence in ways that look "anxious" by Western standards but represent healthy cultural norms.

Cultures valuing emotional restraint may appear "avoidant" but maintain deep connections through action rather than verbal expression.

Example: In Hiroshi's Japanese family, love was shown through careful attention to needs rather than emotional expression. This created secure attachment with a communication style that might appear avoidant in more verbally expressive cultures.

The Spectrum Reality

Most people exhibit a primary attachment style with secondary tendencies (Fraley, 2019). Your attachment style may vary across relationships. You might feel secure with close friends but anxious in romantic relationships, or display avoidant tendencies at work while being securely attached at home (Mikulincer & Shaver, 2023). You might be primarily secure but show anxious patterns during high stress, or undefined avoidant but anxious with specific types of partners.

Our attachment styles aren't fixed but shift based on our circumstances. Current stress levels can transform manageable situations into triggering ones, while our partner's attachment style either amplifies our insecurities or provides a stabilizing influence. The context matters too—we might feel secure with close friends but anxious in new romantic relationships, or confident at work yet vulnerable during family gatherings.

Life transitions like career changes, moves, or loss can temporarily destabilize even secure individuals, causing old patterns to resurface. Cultural and family expectations add another layer, creating tension when our natural attachment needs conflict with what our environment rewards or discourages.

Attachment Style Interactions

Attachment identification involves more than checking boxes on a quiz. Researchby Bartholomew and Horowitz (1991) reveal that attachment exists along two primary dimensions:

1. **Attachment Anxiety**: The degree to which you worry about abandonment, need reassurance, and fear relationship loss.

2. **Attachment Avoidance**: Your comfort level with intimacy, emotional expression, and depending on others. Understanding how different styles interact helps explain relationship dynamics.

The Path Forward

Attachment styles aren't permanent labels, but starting points for growth (Davila & Cobb, 2003). Through conscious awareness, therapeutic work, and corrective relationship experiences, people can develop "earned security"—the ability to form secure relationships regardless of early experiences.

The goal isn't to eliminate your attachment style but to understand it so thoroughly that you can work with it rather than being controlled by it. Each attachment pattern holds an inherent value. Now that we understand the four primary styles, let's explore each. Beginning with anxious attachment—a style characterized by a deep capacity for love and sensitivity to relationship dynamics.

Chapter Three

Anxious Style

You love deeply, completely, with every cell of your being. This depth shapes how you move through relationships, from texting "good morning" to planning date nights and paying attention to every emotional shift. When someone matters to you, they matter. Small moments carry weight: the tone of their voice after work, the time between messages, the warmth in their goodbye kiss.

Your unique sensitivity, a gift that makes you incredibly attuned to relationships, sets you apart. You remember the little details others might miss—their coffee order, the story behind their childhood scar, the way their voice changes when they're holding something back. This same sensitivity means you feel relationship dynamics intensely, reading into the silences and analyzing casual comments for deeper meaning.

Understanding anxious attachment isn't about learning to love less—it's about understanding why you love the way you do. By understanding the impact of experiences, you can build stronger relationships. This capacity for love is your strength, not a weakness.

Understanding Your Inner World

Your body carefully records connection and distance, speaking through physical signals that feel impossible to ignore. Your heart races at an unanswered message, your stomach tightens during conversations about the future, and sleep becomes a distant friend when relationship waters feel uncertain. These responses tell a story your nervous system wrote, which began long before your conscious mind could understand it.

Laura sits next to her partner, watching a movie. They are physically close, but emotionally, she is trying to read the temperature between them. Tonight, his breathing feels different, more distant somehow. Her body responds before her mind can catch up—muscles tensing, breath shortening, attention shifting from the screen to the space between them. These moments reveal how anxiety lives not just in our thoughts but in our very cells, creating a symphony of sensation that carries both warning and wisdom.

The language of anxious attachment speaks through these physical and emotional dialects, turning relationship moments into full-body experiences. A warm good morning text can relieve your system, just as a delayed response can send cortisol[1] racing through your veins. Inner awareness allows mindful responses instead of reactions. For instance, a partner's reaction to a shared accomplishment or behavior during a disagreement can trigger these physical and emotional responses.

---

1. According to the Merriam-Webster, cortisol is hormone produced in the adrenal glands. Cortisol levels can increase in response to stress, both physical and psychological.

Physical Signals

The anxious attachment system activates specific physical responses rooted in survival mechanisms. When relationship security feels threatened, your autonomic nervous system shifts into high alert: heart rate speeds up, breathing becomes shallow, and muscles brace for emotional impact. These reactions aren't random anxiety but your body's learned response to potential relationship threats, shaped by experiences where connection felt unpredictable.

Your nervous system maintains this vigilance through measurable physical changes:

- Cortisol levels rise, triggering that signature chest tightness.

- Sleep becomes disrupted as your brain stays alert for relationship cues.

- Digestion slows as blood flow redirects to muscles and major organs.

- Physical restlessness increases, making it hard to stay present.

- Blood pressure elevates, creating that familiar tension headache.

These physiological responses mirror actual physical danger. Your body treats an emotional threat as seriously as a physical threat, which explains why relationship stress often feels so physically demanding. Your system is preparing for survival.

The exact mechanisms that once protected you from childhood emotional harm now activate during adult relationship uncertainty. These bodily responses then create a feedback loop with your emotional system. Each physical sensation, such as a racing heart or tense muscles, can amplify relationship anxiety. The heightened emotional state intensifies physical symptoms, creating a cycle of heightened sensitivity and reactivity.

Emotional Intensity

One text from your partner saying, "We need to talk," alters your whole emotional world. Your heart races, thoughts spiral, and suddenly, that deadline at work becomes completely irrelevant compared to decoding what those four words might mean. Relationship signals overload the anxious brain, triggering quick emotional responses.

The intensity shows up in predictable ways, including some or all of:

- A warm message floods you with relief.

- Minor disagreements feel like relationship threats.

- Casual comments need careful analysis.

- Distance, even brief, creates immediate unease.

- Others' moods directly affect your emotional state.

Why these? Because your brain learns at a very early stage to alert you to emotional changes. When your partner seems distant during dinner, you feel it in your chest before you can name it; when they're late without texting, your mood drops before logic can step in with reasonable explanations.

Science explains this as a highly tuned threat-detection system. Still, the lived experience feels more immediate: emotions wash through you in powerful waves, each relationship moment carrying the weight of the past and future combined. You react this way not because you choose to but because your brain learned that staying alert to connection keeps you safe.

Thought Patterns

Your mind moves in well-worn paths when it comes to love and connection. A simple "I need space" from your partner launches a cascade of thoughts: they're pulling away, you've done something wrong, and the relationship must be in trouble. Each delayed response or brief interaction proves that your anxious mind is building without your permission.

The thoughts loop in familiar patterns:

- "They're distant today," becomes "They're losing interest."

- "I should give them space," turns into "If I pull back, they might leave."

- "Something feels off," spirals into relationship disaster scenarios.

- "They're busy at work," transforms into "I'm not a priority."

The anxious mind excels at connecting dots that aren't there, creating stories from fragments of information. A partner's quiet mood spawns theories about relationship satisfaction. Their friendly chat with a coworker becomes a potential competition for their affection. Each casual interaction carries the weight of the relationship's future. You're not alone in this struggle with overthinking. Many others with anxious attachment styles share this experience.

Your brain runs these calculations automatically, like a supercomputer dedicated to relationship math. Every message gets analyzed, every interaction evaluated, every silence filled with meaning. Not because you choose to overthink, but because your mind learned early that missing relationship signals could mean losing connection.

Relationship Dynamics

This book explores loving and being loved by anxious partners. Some of the standout responses revealed three distinct dynamics that consistently emerge:

Dynamic 1: When you love someone, they become the center of your universe.

Anxious attachment brings a particular devotion to relationships. You notice everything about your person—their subtle mood shifts, small gestures, and unspoken needs. This attention creates a deep connection but can also feel heavy, especially when everyday actions carry the weight of relationship security.

Dynamic 2: You find yourself constantly proving your love.

The need for consistent reassurance creates a unique relationship rhythm. Words of love require frequent renewal, casual distance needs a quick repair, and regular relationship fluctuations demand extra attention. These feelings aren't about neediness—it's about your attachment system requiring regular connection confirmation.

Dynamic 3: You try so hard to keep them close that sometimes it pushes them away.

The behaviors meant to secure connection—frequent checking in, seeking reassurance, monitoring for changes—can create the distance they intend to prevent.

None of these patterns exist to shame or label. Instead, they illuminate how early attachment experiences shape adult relationships and offer a map for understanding why we love the way we do.

The Attraction Dynamics of Anxious Attacment

Love has a certain gravity when one is anxiously attached. Research reveals consistent patterns in who anxious hearts attract and why these attractions feel so magnetic. These patterns aren't random; they reflect deeper attachment needs and early relationship blueprints.

The Avoidant Pull

The most potent attraction often forms with avoidant partners, creating what therapists call the anxious-avoidant trap. The dynamic feels eerily familiar: You reach out, they step back; they come close; you want closer; they need space, and you feel abandoned. This pattern recreates early relationship dynamics where love felt just out of reach. The avoidant partner's emotional distance triggers your deepest attachment wounds, making the connection feel more intense, critical, and authentic.

The Inconsistent Charmer

Another common attraction forms with partners who show unpredictable patterns of attention and affection: incredibly present one day, distant the next. Their warmth feels intoxicating but needs to be more reliable. They might text constantly for days, then disappear without explanation. This inconsistency triggers your attachment system's hypervigilance, keeping you alert and invested, always working to maintain a connection.

Drawn to the Secure

Sometimes, anxious attachment leads to secure partners, but this connection often feels foreign initially. You're not used to their consistency, which might seem boring compared to the dramatic highs and lows you're used to. Their emotional availability might make you uncomfortable, triggering fears about what happens when the other shoe drops. While less intense initially, these offer the best opportunity for developing earned secure attachment.

These patterns don't define your relationship destiny. You're more likely to repeat similar relationship dynamics until you recognize why certain partners feel so irresistible. With awareness comes choice—choosing partners based on their capacity for consistent connection rather than their ability to trigger familiar attachment wounds.

The Brightside

The mistake we often make is focusing too much on the negative aspects of our attachment styles, but anxious attachment carries unique gifts that make relationships more profound. Your sensitivity to emotional nuance lets you pick up on subtle shifts in others' feelings, making you exceptionally attuned to those you care about.

Research by Simpson et al. (2007) found that anxiously attached individuals show superior accuracy in reading others' emotional states, particularly negative emotions. This skill serves relationships well when channeled appropriately. This emotional intelligence shows up in countless ways—noticing when a friend needs support before they say anything. Or, sensing when your partner has had a rough day just from their breathing, and knowing what someone needs in moments of distress.

Your capacity for empathy and deep connection creates relationships of extraordinary depth. You remember the small details that make others feel genuinely seen: the name of your colleague's sick pet, your friend's coffee preference, the story behind your partner's childhood scar. The attention to detail makes people feel noticed, loved, cared for, and understood.

That same intensity that makes uncertainty challenging also makes you an incredibly loyal and dedicated partner. When you commit, you commit fully; you show up consistently, make time for meaningful conversations, and prioritize emotional intimacy. Your willingness to address relationship issues head-on, though sometimes driven by anxiety, often leads to deeper understanding and stronger bonds. This courage to engage and lead with emotional complexity makes you a great friend, partner, daughter, and sibling, so cherish those qualities about you.

Practical Tools and Strategies

It's simple to believe that's just who you are, but to cultivate a healthy and secure love; you must commit to self-improvement. Growth starts with small steps that feel uncomfortable initially, like learning to sit with uncertainty without sending that third text or practicing self-soothing when your partner needs space. Working toward secure attachment isn't about changing who you are or dampening your capacity to love deeply.

Building Communication Skills

Anxious attachment often speaks in roundabout ways—hinting at needs, hoping others will read between the lines, or staying quiet until emotions overflow. Clear communication feels risky when you're used to editing yourself to keep others close. Yet, learning to express needs directly while staying connected to yourself transforms relationship dynamics.

Direct Expression

Replace indirect communication with explicit statements:

- Instead of "It's fine," when it isn't, try "I'm feeling hurt and need to talk about it."

- Rather than dropping hints, name your needs: "I'd love to spend one-on-one time with you this weekend."

- Rephrase "Maybe we could..." as "I'd prefer...".

Express appreciation directly instead of assuming it's understood.

Don't Bottle Your Anxiety

Let your partner know when anxiety speaks.

"I know this might be anxiety talking, but I need to share what I'm feeling."

"When you were quiet today, my mind created stories. Can you help me understand what's actually happening?"

Setting Boundaries

Boundaries feel incredibly challenging with anxious attachment—fear of loss makes it tempting to accept any treatment. Practice:

- Stating limits before resentment builds.

- Expressing what you need rather than what you don't want.

- Being consistent with your boundaries.

- Recognizing that healthy boundaries strengthen rather than threaten connections.

The Check-In Framework

Regular relationship check-ins prevent anxiety from building:

- Schedule regular times to discuss relationship needs

- Share appreciation before diving into concerns

- Use "I feel" statements rather than accusations

- Listen to understand rather than wait to respond

- Express needs clearly without apologizing for having them

This communication framework creates space for both security and growth. The goal isn't perfect communication but authentic expression that brings you closer to genuine connection rather than anxious attachment's familiar dance of hint and hope.

We can practice all the modalities and learn all the interventions, but nothing will ever replace the power of meeting yourself in your humanity. Your anxious attachment didn't develop overnight—it grew from actual experiences, real hurts, and genuine moments when the connection felt uncertain. The intensity of your feelings isn't wrong. Your need for reassurance isn't a character flaw. Your deep capacity for love isn't something to fix.

Remember, this work isn't about becoming different or learning to need less. It's about adding new tools to your emotional toolkit and expressing love so that they feel both authentic to you and sustainable in relationships. Sometimes, you'll slip back into old patterns—that's not failure; it's being human. The goal isn't perfect attachment, but growing awareness and gentle shifts toward security, one small, brave choice at a time.

Chapter Four

Avoidant Style

The Paradox of Independence

W hen David receives a text saying "We need to talk," his first instinct isn't curiosity—it's strategy. His mind immediately begins calculating escape routes: *Can this wait until tomorrow? Maybe I should work* late tonight. *What if I suggest we discuss it over* dinner, *where emotional* intensity feels *less likely?* This isn't callousness; it's the sophisticated defense system of avoidant attachment, where emotional conversations trigger the same fight-or-flight responses others might feel facing physical danger.

For avoidantly attached individuals, relationships exist in a delicate balance between connection and self-protection. They genuinely care about their partners, but struggle with the vulnerability that deep intimacy requires. Understanding avoidant attachment means recognizing that beneath the apparent emotional distance lies not indifference, but a nervous system that learned early to equate emotional exposure to danger.

This chapter explores the internal world of avoidant attachment—not just how it appears to others, but how it feels from the inside. We'll examine adaptive strategies that once provided protection, and most importantly, how avoidantly attached individuals can maintain their autonomy while building the connections they secretly crave.

Emotional Distancing in Relationships

People emotionally distance themselves in relationships when they feel too naked, too vulnerable, too close, too stripped away of their independence. Jessica and Ryan met on a dating app that supposedly matched traits, but their personalities were worlds apart. Jess runs a successful art gallery, fills her Instagram with color studies and exhibition openings, and talks about feelings like they're old friends. While Ryan analyzes market trends for a living, he approaches problems with spreadsheet precision. He keeps his emotional world as ordered as his stock portfolio.

Their early connection was intense—the classic pull between an emotional explorer and a careful navigator of feelings. However, as their relationship deepens, Ryan's avoidant patterns emerge clearly. He excels at the practical side of love: planning dates, remembering her coffee order, and showing up on time. Yet when Jess brings up emotional topics—their future, her deeper feelings, concerns about their connection—his first instinct is to create distance. He responds to emotional questions with logical answers, meets vulnerability with analysis, and turns heart matters into head matters.

His response isn't about lack of care; Ryan feels deeply for Jess. But his relationship to emotional intimacy follows old, ingrained patterns: He deflects when feelings get too intense, retreats when connection threatens independence, and maintains control when vulnerability looms. These responses stem from early lessons about love and safety, where keeping emotional distance meant securing the ground beneath his feet.

Reduced Emotional Availability

Emotional availability forms the foundation of intimate relationships. It's the capacity to show up for your partner in ways beyond physical presence—or turning toward your partner when they share the good news, offering comfort when distressed, and staying present during tough conversations instead of reaching for distractions. In contrast, an emotionally available partner responds to "I had a rough day" with attention and empathy rather than solutions or silence.

When avoidant patterns take hold, this emotional presence dims. You might still sit next to your partner on the couch, but your mind wanders to work emails while they share their fears about a family situation. You offer logical solutions instead of understanding. Although physical intimacy continues, emotional intimacy feels increasingly difficult to maintain.

Signs include using a phone during conversations, emotional avoidance, practical advice instead of empathy, busy schedules, and withdrawing from a partner's needs.

For Ryan and Jess, this pattern plays out in subtle ways. When Jess shares her excitement about a new exhibition, Ryan responds with questions about logistics and sales projections rather than connecting with her enthusiasm. She reaches for emotional intimacy. Yet, he goes for his phone, creating a dance of connection and disconnection that leaves both feeling unseen in different ways. Their story reflects a common challenge: learning to bridge the gap between being physically present and emotionally available, between caring profoundly and showing it in ways that matter.

We cultivate emotional availability through conscious effort and intentional actions. It's about catching yourself when your mind wanders during meaningful conversations, putting down your phone when your partner wants to talk, and staying present with them, even through uncomfortable emotions, instead of deflecting or avoiding them. It's about responding to emotional bids with presence rather than distance.

These small, consistent practices genuinely matter.

- Making eye contact during conversations.

- Asking questions about feelings rather than just facts.

- Sharing your own emotional experiences, even briefly.

- Acknowledging your partner's emotions before offering solutions.

- Creating dedicated time for deeper conversations.

These aren't complicated; they ensure your partner feels seen, loved, cherished, and held in your presence.

Intimacy

You could ask twenty people what intimacy means to them. The answers will be deeply moving because they reveal something distinct about humanity, something that says. Despite our differences, being known is the best way to be loved.

Some answers will be like these:

- "Intimacy is when I can tell you about my day without editing out the messy parts."

- "It's being able to sit in silence and feel completely at home."

- "When I can cry without explaining why and you don't try to fix it."

- "Knowing someone sees all my cracks and stays, anyway."

- "The moment in between 'I need to tell you something' and actually telling you—and feeling safe in that space."

For the avoidant heart, this closeness, this proximity, this sharing of hearts and souls often triggers an internal alarm system within the nervous system; the closer someone gets to you, the more vulnerable you feel, while the more vulnerable you feel, the stronger your urge to create distance. It's not about the ability to love—it's about a nervous system trained to equate intimacy with danger.

The pull-back often surfaces when a partner leans on you emotionally, shares deep feelings, or when the relationship heads toward commitment. Your mind crafts exit strategies in advance while your heart keeps strict emotional boundaries.

Emotional intimacy, unlike physical, feels unstable and less defined.

Resisting intimacy prevents healing from the fear of vulnerability. Avoidant challenge is to lean into vulnerability rather than pull away when connections intensify.

Impact on Relationship Dynamics

Consider this conversation that transpired between Jess and Ryan:

Jess: "I feel like every time I try to get closer, you find a way to create distance."

Ryan: "I don't see it that way. I'm here, aren't I?"

Jess: "Physically, yes. But emotionally... it's like trying to hug a wall sometimes."

Ryan: "That's not fair. Just because I don't process things the same way you do—"

Jess: "It's not about processing. It's about showing up. Like last week, when I told you about my mom's diagnosis, you immediately started researching treatment options instead of just... being there."

Ryan: "I was trying to help. What's wrong with wanting to solve the problem?"

Jess: "Nothing's wrong with it. But sometimes I don't need solutions. I just need you to sit with me during the hard stuff."

This typical interaction might occur with an avoidant partner. One partner reaches for a deeper connection while the other retreats into practicality and problem-solving. The avoidant partner isn't deliberately distant or cruel—for that matter, they're responding most naturally and safely, through action rather than emotion, solutions rather than presence. These patterns create a particular distance in relationships, where one partner constantly moves toward emotion while the other moves toward logic, creating a wider disconnect with each interaction.

Relationship safety (emotional and physical) is fundamental; without it, intimacy is impossible.

This wall might be invisible, but its presence shapes every interaction, every connection attempt, and every possibility for deeper intimacy. The work is to keep these walls intact and to create enough safety so that both partners can slowly and carefully begin to lower their defenses.

Creating Safe Spaces

Avoidant partners need safety in their relationships as well. Consider these ideas:

- "Safety means knowing I can take space without being made to feel guilty about it."

- "When my partner accepts that, sometimes I need to process things alone first."

- "Not being pushed to share before I'm ready."

- "When they understand that, my need for independence isn't a rejection of them."

- "Safety is knowing they won't read into every silence or need for space."

- "When they don't take my way of showing love personally."

- "Having a partner who gives me time to warm up to emotional conversations."

- "Not being labeled as 'cold' or 'distant' when I'm just being myself."

These ideas reveal something crucial about creating safety for avoidant partners: it's not just about the presence of certain behaviors but the absence of pressure. Avoidant partners need relationships where independence poses no threat to intimacy, where taking space doesn't trigger pursuit, and where others respect their often slower and more internal emotional processing instead of criticizing it.

Practical Strategies

Creating safety in relationships with avoidant partners requires deliberate care and attention. These strategies emerged from countless conversations with couples who've learned to dance with distance and closeness:

Time-Boxing Emotional Conversations

Agree on specific timeframes instead of diving into marathon discussions about feelings or relationship status. "Can we talk about this for twenty minutes?" feels more manageable than an open-ended emotional exploration. Thus, creating content that helps avoidant partners stay present rather than feeling overwhelmed or trapped.

Structured Check-Ins

Create regular but predictable moments of connection. A Sunday morning coffee ritual, a weekly walk, or an end-of-day debrief can become safe containers for sharing. When emotional connection becomes part of a routine, it feels less threatening and more natural. The key lies in consistency without pressure, knowing these moments exist but not forcing depth when it doesn't feel right.

Physical-Emotional Balance

Many avoidant partners find physical touch easier than verbal emotional expression. Simple practices like holding hands during hard conversations, sitting close while watching TV, or sharing physical space while doing separate activities can create security without overwhelming the system. This allows connection to build through comfortable channels rather than pushing immediately for emotional vulnerability.

The Permission to Retreat

Explicitly agree that taking space is healthy and allowed. Create clear signals for when an avoidant partner needs to step back—maybe a specific phrase or gesture that communicates, "I need some time," without triggering abandonment fears in the partner. This permission to retreat makes it safer to stay connected.

Overcoming Emotional Withdrawal

People withdraw emotionally because, somewhere along the way, they learn that feelings are either too big to handle or too dangerous to show. The child whose tears met silence learned to swallow them. The teenager whose anger was punished learned to freeze it. The young adult, whose expressions of love were met with emotional distance, gradually learned to suppress and dim their feelings. These early lessons create a particular kind of emotional muscle memory that automatically pulls back when feelings grow intense.

Steps to Overcome Emotional Withdrawal

Staying emotionally present when every instinct says run requires patience, practice, and, most importantly, self-compassion. These three key areas create a foundation for changing long-held patterns of withdrawal.

Connect: Connection starts with yourself before it can extend to others. Learning to sit with your emotions without immediately shutting them down or solving them. Begin with small moments—notice how your body feels when emotions arise, observe your automatic response to pull away, and practice staying present for thirty seconds longer than you feel comfortable. Like building muscle, emotional presence grows stronger with consistent, gentle exercise.

Emotionally regulate: Your nervous system needs new data about emotional safety. Start by tracking your withdrawal triggers: what situations, words, or actions send you reaching for emotional escape routes? Understanding these patterns helps you respond rather than react. Simple practices like deep breathing or grounding exercises give you tools to stay present when emotions intensify. The goal is to build your capacity to function alongside it.

Learn to communicate: Communication often feels safer when it follows clear structures. Practice expressing feelings in small, manageable doses using simple formats: "When [situation] happens, I feel [emotion]" or "I need [specific request]." Start with low-stakes conversations where emotional risk feels minimal. Share observations about daily events before moving to deeper feelings. Let others know when you need to pause and process. Consider saying, "I want to think about this and come back to our conversation later," to create a space without complete withdrawal.

Avoidance in Family Relationships

Family dinner tables tell stories about attachment while the teenager escapes to their room. When plates are cleared, the father shows love through actions but never words, and the mother cleans up to avoid deeper conversations. These patterns of connection and distance echo through generations, creating familiar dances of approach and retreat in family systems.

Maya describes Sunday dinners at her parents' house: "Dad's always been...present but not present. He focuses on tasks, ignoring emotional needs. Suddenly, he needs to check something in the garage." Years later, Maya catches herself in the same pattern with her children, showing up for every soccer game but freezing when they need emotional support.

The language of avoidance speaks clearly in family relationships. It sounds like "I'm fine" when you're not, looks like empty chairs at emotional moments, and feels like love expressed through tasks instead of touch. These families often run smoothly on the surface—homework gets checked, meals appear on time, and houses stay in perfect order. But beneath this well-orchestrated dance of daily life runs a quieter current: the subtle ways each generation learns to keep their hearts safe by keeping others at a careful distance.

How Patterns Show Up

To understand how avoidance shapes families, we must look beyond the apparent distance to the subtle ways it influences everyday interactions. Patterns emerge that show how avoidant attachment passes through generations, creating specific behaviors that protect against emotional closeness while maintaining the appearance of family harmony.

Daily Rhythms and Routines

Avoidance first manifests in how families structure their time. Instead of natural flows of togetherness and separation, avoidant families create rigid schedules that limit spontaneous interaction. Parents might work late consistently, not just because of career demands but because it provides a legitimate buffer against evening emotional connection. Children learn to time their appearances around these patterns—coming down for dinner just as it ends, doing homework behind closed doors, and scheduling activities that minimize family time.

Communication Patterns

Information moves through avoidant families according to distinct rules. Meaningful conversations happen via text because they offer emotional distance. Family members perfect the art of deflection: "How are you?" is answered with facts about the day's activities rather than feelings.

When emotions surface, avoidant family members employ specific strategies: changing the subject, bringing up practical matters, or physically leaving the space.

Watch how a teenage son responds to his mother's concern about his recent withdrawal—he'll likely offer information about grades or sports instead of his emotional state.

Crisis Management

Family difficulties most clearly reveal avoidant patterns. When the grandmother gets sick, family members show up with practical help, organizing medical appointments, handling insurance, and arranging meals. But emotional support remains notably absent. No one sits with the grief, shares fears, or discusses feelings about potential loss. The family coordinates care through spreadsheets and schedules while emotions remain unspoken. It's a learned response where doing feels safer than feeling but is perceived as negligence.

Rebuilding Family Connections

Families that successfully navigate avoidant patterns share stories not of dramatic transformations but of small, intentional shifts that fade their family landscape. Their experiences reveal patterns of growth that others can learn from, showing how connection rebuilds not through force but through gentle, consistent change.

Healing happens in small, meaningful moments: a father stays present with his daughter's tears; a mother says, "I missed you," instead of the usual, "Did you remember your jacket?"; and siblings learn to share space in silence, with no constant noise or activity.

These aren't dramatic breakthroughs but quiet choices that, over time, create new connection patterns.

What Works:

- Regular, time-limited family meetings with clear agendas.

- Shared activities that allow parallel play—cooking together, gardening, and home projects.

- Creating specific times for checking in, making connections predictable rather than invasive.

- Building new traditions that balance togetherness with personal space.

- Using technology thoughtfully—group chats for sharing daily moments, not just logistics.

The Role of Professional Support

Sometimes, families need a guide in this territory. Family therapy offers a contained space to practice new patterns. The right therapist acts like a translator between family members' different emotional languages, helping each person feel understood while learning to understand others. They can teach specific tools for:

- Expressing needs without triggering defensive responses.

- Recognizing when avoidance is happening.

- Creating safety for vulnerability.

- Respecting boundaries while building connections.

Chapter Five

Disorganized Style

When Elena tries to describe her relationships, words feel in adequate. "I want closeness so desperately that it physically hurts," she explains, "but the moment someone gets too close, I panic and push them away. Then I hate myself for pushing away the very thing I want most." This internal contradiction—simultaneously reaching for and rejecting connection—captures the essence of disorganized attachment, where love and fear become so intertwined that they feel indistinguishable.

The Hidden Struggle

Disorganized attachment represents the most complex and least understood attachment pattern, affecting approximately 5-10% of the general population but up to 80% of those with trauma histories (van der Kolk, 2021). Unlike other attachment styles that develop coherent relationship strategies, disorganized attachment creates a perfect storm of contradictory impulses that generate internal chaos and unpredictable relationship behaviors.

To understand disorganized attachment, we must recognize it as the nervous system's creative response to an impossible situation: when the person meant to provide safety becomes the source of fear.

This exploration examines the neurobiological foundations of this complex pattern, its manifestations across different life domains, and most importantly, the pathways toward integration and healing.

The Inner Contradiction

Disorganized attachment often feels like chaos inside both mind and body—a simultaneous pull toward and retreat from intimacy. While anxious attachment seeks connection and avoidant attachment maintains distance, disorganized attachment swings chaotically between both extremes, creating relationship patterns that feel impossible to break.

This attachment style is characterized by a conflicting desire for closeness paired with an overwhelming fear of that very connection. Individuals display inconsistent or contradictory behaviors in relationships, such as seeking comfort from someone they simultaneously perceive as a source of fear or distress. This pattern typically stems from early caregiving experiences where a caregiver served as both protector and threat—offering comfort one moment and creating fear the next through abuse, neglect, or unpredictable behavior.

What It Looks Like in Daily Life

The core of disorganized attachment lives in a deep sense of unworthiness—a bone-deep certainty that something about you is fundamentally wrong. When your partner expresses love, their words bounce off walls built from experiences that taught you love either hurts or disappears. You might achieve great things, help everyone around you, and excel in your career, yet still feel like you're fooling everyone who claims to care about you.

When someone says "I love you," your first instinct is to search their face for lies. Love feels like a trap, a trick, or a test you're destined to fail. Your brain has learned to treat affection with suspicion because it historically came with conditions or consequences. This creates a painful paradox where you desperately want to believe in love while simultaneously being convinced it can't be genuine—at least not for you.

Your attention becomes a constant radar for rejection, scanning every interaction for signs of abandonment. A delayed text response feels like proof they're pulling away. A slight change in tone signals the beginning of the end. Even genuine care gets processed as potential manipulation because somewhere along the way, you learned that love and harm often wear the same face.

The Path Forward

Despite its complexity, disorganized attachment is not a life sentence. Individuals with this attachment style can work toward healthier patterns through therapy, self-awareness, and consistent, safe relationships. The journey involves learning to recognize these contradictory impulses, understanding their origins, and gradually building tolerance for the vulnerability that genuine connection requires.

Understanding disorganized attachment is the first step toward healing—recognizing that these responses aren't character flaws but adaptive strategies developed in impossible circumstances. With patience, support, and the right therapeutic approach, it becomes possible to move toward more secure and stable relationship patterns.

Core Dynamics and Behaviors

Emily is eight years old again, standing in her childhood kitchen. The air feels thick with something she can't name while her father's footsteps echo down the hall. Some days, these footsteps meant ice cream after dinner; other days, they carried storms. Her mother's face would shift too: warm and present one moment, blank and unreachable the next. Twenty years later, Emily still carries this uncertainty in her bones. Love feels like a language where the words keep changing meaning.

Now, at thirty-two, her relationships follow a painful pattern. She falls hard and fast, then sabotages the connection before it can hurt her. She craves intimacy with an intensity that scares her partners, then disappears when they move closer. In couples therapy, she describes feeling like two different people: one desperate for love, the other sure it will destroy her.

Disorganized attachment occurs when the heart learns conflicting withdrawal from lessons about love early on. When caregivers become a source of comfort and fear, the brain creates complex survival strategies. It's not a choice or a flaw; it's what happens when love and danger live too close, trust becomes a gamble rather than a given, and the people meant to protect you become unpredictable forces in your emotional world.

Common behaviors include:

- Craving intimacy but fearing vulnerability

- Sudden emotional shifts: warmth one moment, withdrawal from the next

- Difficulty regulating emotions

- Hypervigilance toward perceived threats or rejection

- Frequent self-sabotaging behavior in relationships

These behaviors reflect deeply ingrained survival strategies formed in environments marked by trauma, neglect, or inconsistent care.

Case Studies

Emily: The Ambivalent Partner

Emily, a 32-year-old graphic designer, described her relationship history as "intense but short-lived." She would bond quickly, feel euphoric about a new connection, then suddenly experience dread and withdraw. In therapy, she traced these patterns back to her childhood. Her mother had struggled with addiction, alternating between affection and outbursts. Emily's nervous system associated closeness with unpredictability, making her feel unsafe in intimacy.

Emily tells a friend about some of the previous relationships she'd had. The one that stood out in her mind was with Brad. "I met him at a friend's party, and within weeks, I was convinced he was my soulmate." "I'd text him these long messages about how much he meant to me, then panic and block his number before he could respond. I'd show up at his apartment wanting to spend the night, then get overwhelmed by his closeness and leave at 3 A.M. without explanation."

Their eight-month relationship became a cycle of intense connection, followed by sudden withdrawals. Emily shares her deepest secrets one day, then accuses Brad of using them against her the next day. She'd plan their future together undefined, then disappear for weeks when he showed genuine interest in those plans.

"The worst part," she admits, "was that the better he treated me, the more I wanted to run. When he was distant, I'd chase him desperately, but his kindness felt like a trap I needed to escape."

Andre: The Push-Pull Dynamic

Andre, a 40-year-old school counselor, noticed a pattern in his romantic life: he often felt compelled to "test" his partners' loyalty, starting arguments or threatening to leave even when things were stable. These tests were rooted in childhood experiences with a parent who was physically present but emotionally volatile.

During arguments, Andre would raise his voice to protect himself, while his partners became overwhelmed and disengaged. Neither felt heard nor understood, and conflicts spiraled into hurt rather than resolution. Andre worked with an Internal Family System (IFS) therapist to identify and comfort his "protector" parts that emerged during intimacy. This inner dialogue helped him reduce conflict-driven patterns.

Casey: Navigating Friendship with Disorganized Attachment

Casey, a non-binary college student, experienced similar push-pull behaviors in friendships. They often ghosted friends after revealing personal information, fearing later rejection or ridicule. Casey found themselves intensely drawn to new friends but also felt overwhelming anxiety when relationships deepened. They feared being left behind but also struggled to fully open up, creating cycles of emotional highs and lows.

With the support of a trauma-informed group therapy program, Casey practiced naming and expressing fears in real-time. Over time, this improved their ability to sustain vulnerability in peer relationships and reduced the tendency to disappear when connections felt too intense.

Behavioral Traits

Disorganized attachment emerges from a lack of consistency in early caregiving, where caregivers were simultaneously a source of comfort and fear. This creates confusion about how relationships work and whether they can be trusted. Five key traits often define this attachment style:

Fear of Abandonment and Intimacy

Disorganized attachment creates a paradox: craving intimacy but fearing the required vulnerability. Relationships may feel like a battlefield where every connection risks emotional injury. This fear may lead to inconsistent behaviors, such as clinging to a partner one moment and withdrawing the next to protect oneself.

Emotional Dysregulation

Emotions often feel like an untamed storm—intense, unpredictable, and challenging to control. People with disorganized attachment may experience emotional outbursts or sudden emotional shutdowns, unable to navigate their feelings stably. This emotional volatility often stems from an inability to process or express emotions safely because of experiences of invalidation or neglect.

Difficulty Trusting Others

Trust becomes a fragile concept for those with disorganized attachment. Early caregivers who were both comforting and frightening created an association between closeness and danger. As a result, trusting others often feels risky. This lack of trust can lead to hypervigilance, over-analyzing behaviors, or self-sabotaging relationships to avoid perceived risks.

Conflicted Responses to Boundaries

Boundaries can feel threatening, as they may trigger fears of abandonment or rejection. People with disorganized attachment may struggle to set boundaries, fearing that doing so will alienate others. Learning to see boundaries as bridges rather than walls is crucial in healing and creating healthier relational dynamics.

Conflict in Relationships

Disorganized attachment often turns conflict into chaos. Rather than seeing disagreements as opportunities for growth, individuals may view them as threats to the relationship's stability. Fear of rejection may lead to overreacting, shutting down, or blaming others.

The Role of Past Trauma

If you boil down the essence of disorganized attachment, trauma lies at its core. It's not always the big, obvious kind that makes headlines, but often the quiet, persistent type that occurs in ordinary homes, where a child learns that the same hands offering comfort might also bring harm and where love and fear become inseparably intertwined.

Think of your nervous system as a security system that learned conflicting information early on when danger and safety wore the same face. Perhaps a parent who could be loving one moment and frightening the next, or a caregiver who met needs with unpredictable responses. Your brain couldn't create clear categories for what's safe and what isn't, so instead, it learned to stay alert to everything and treat love and threats as potential partners rather than opposites.

These early experiences write themselves into your body's operating manual, creating automatic responses that might not make sense now but were essential for survival then. This could be tensing up when someone hugs you even while craving their touch or feeling panic rise when a partner expresses love, as your system is confused about whether to melt or flee. These aren't character flaws or conscious choices, but protective patterns programmed by experiences where attachment figures were simultaneously sources of comfort and fear.

Healing becomes possible when we recognize that these responses made perfect sense in their original context. Your brain did what it needed to help you survive confusing and sometimes dangerous early relationships. As an adult, you can begin teaching your nervous system new patterns—but this process requires patience, understanding, and often professional support.

Understanding the Core Dynamics

Disorganized attachment differs from **anxious** and **avoidant attachment styles** in significant ways, primarily because of the conflicting emotional experiences and behaviors it represents. Here's a breakdown of the differences:

Fear of Intimacy vs. Desire for Connection

- **Anxious Attachment:** Individuals crave closeness and intimacy but fear rejection or abandonment. They may become clingy, overly dependent, or preoccupied with the relationship to gain reassurance.

- **Avoidant Attachment:** Individuals value independence and often suppress their need for connection. They may avoid closeness or push people away to maintain emotional distance, feeling uncomfortable with vulnerability.

- **Disorganized Attachment:** Individuals experience a combination of both: they want intimacy, is challenging but are also afraid of it. This push-pull dynamic creates confusion, as they may seek closeness but pull away out of fear, leading to erratic or contradictory behaviors.

Root Cause

- **Anxious Attachment:** Often stems from inconsistent caregiving, where emotional needs were sometimes met and ignored.

- **Avoidant Attachment:** It often develops when caregivers are emotionally unavailable or dismissive, teaching the child to suppress their need for emotional connection.

- **Disorganized Attachment:** It commonly arises in environments where caregivers are both a source of comfort and fear, such as in cases of abuse, neglect, or unpredictable behavior. The child experiences conflicting messages: "I need you, but I'm afraid of you."

Emotional Regulation

- **Anxious Attachment:** Individuals struggle with managing their emotions, often becoming overwhelmed by their fear of being abandoned.

- **Avoidant Attachment:** Individuals avoid emotional expression, suppressing their feelings to maintain control and independence.

- **Disorganized Attachment:** Emotional regulation is challenging. Individuals may swing between extremes—overwhelmed by emotions undefined and shutting down at others.

Relational Patterns

- **Anxious Attachment:** Highly dependent on partners for validation, often overthinking or doubting the relationship.

- **Avoidant Attachment:** Struggles with vulnerability and prefers to keep relationships at arm's length, prioritizing self-reliance.

- **Disorganized Attachment:** Exhibits contradictory behaviors: seeking closeness while sabotaging relationships out of fear or mistrust. These individuals may display erratic behaviors, such as emotional outbursts or sudden withdrawal.

The major difference between anxious and avoidant styles is **the conflict between wanting and fearing connection**, which often leads to chaotic or unpredictable relationship patterns. While anxious and avoidant styles may consistently lean toward one behavior (seeking or avoiding closeness), disorganized attachment fluctuates between extremes.

The Path to Healing

Healing from disorganized attachment involves untangling the contradictory feelings of love and fear. With time, individuals can learn to:

- Build trust through safe, consistent relationships

- Regulate emotions with mindfulness or therapeutic techniques

- Set and respect boundaries without fear of rejection

- Recognize and change the internal narratives that create self-doubt

Secure relationships, whether with a partner, therapist, or friend, can serve as a corrective experience, teaching that connection can be safe, stable, and nourishing.

Healing from disorganized attachment is a nonlinear journey. It requires understanding and soothing the parts of ourselves that carry fear from the past while nurturing the capacity for trust and connection in the present. The goal is not perfection, but emotional integration—a stable inner world that supports sustainable intimacy.

We can spend our whole lives trying to understand patterns that seem beyond our control, why love feels like oxygen and poison, safety and danger, home and exile. But healing doesn't require you to become someone new or erase the experiences that shaped you. It only asks you to see your patterns compassionately and understand that your reactions—however chaotic they might seem—were once necessary survival strategies.

Growth stems from small acts of presence, courage, and belief. Even when it feels overwhelming, your capacity for deep feeling is also your pathway to profound connection. The same sensitivity that makes you vulnerable to pain also allows you to experience love with extraordinary depth.

Disorganized attachment reflects a conflicted inner world in which the desire for connection conflicts with the fear of being hurt. This attachment style often develops from inconsistent, frightening, or neglectful early caregiving experiences. While relationships may feel chaotic or unpredictable, healing is possible with self-awareness, therapy, and supportive connections. Over time, individuals can rewrite their attachment story, creating pathways to trust, emotional stability, and authentic connection.

A Self-Assessment Tool

Determining whether your attachment style is disorganized or simply a combination of anxious and avoidant patterns can be tricky. While only a mental health professional can adequately assess, these questions might help you recognize disorganized attachment patterns in your relationships. Take a moment to reflect on each question, noting which responses feel familiar.

Relationship Patterns:

- Do you intensely crave relationships but feel terrified when you get close to someone?

- Have you been told your behavior in relationships is unpredictable or confusing?

- Do you alternate between pursuing people intensely and pushing them away aggressively?

- Is it common for you to desperately need and deeply distrust the same person?

Emotional Responses:

- Do you find yourself feeling both loving and fearful toward your partner simultaneously?

- Do you feel drawn to and threatened by someone showing genuine care?

- Are your emotional reactions often intense and seemingly contradictory?

- Do you struggle to make sense of your feelings in relationships?

Past Experiences:

- Are your childhood memories either extremely vivid or strangely blank?

- Did you grow up feeling that love and fear were closely connected?

- Was there a time when those meant to protect you also caused you distress?

- Do you need help forming a coherent narrative about your early relationships?

Suppose you answer yes to many of these questions, particularly those related to contradictory responses to love and feelings of attraction and aversion to intimacy. In that case, you might be experiencing patterns of disorganized attachment. Remember: This isn't a diagnostic tool but a starting point for better understanding yourself and potentially seeking professional support.

Therapeutic Approaches Beyond CBT

While Cognitive Behavioral Therapy (CBT) is helpful for recognizing distorted thinking patterns, disorganized attachment often requires deeper, trauma-sensitive methods to access the emotional core of attachment fear. Here are several complementary approaches that have shown particular effectiveness:

1. Internal Family Systems (IFS)

IFS views the self as composed of parts—some protective, some wounded. This approach helps disorganized individuals connect with the part of themselves that fears intimacy and the part that longs for it. By helping these parts speak safely, individuals experience internal coherence and reduce relational chaos.

In practice, this might involve identifying your "protector" part that creates distance when someone gets too close, and your "exile" part that holds the original wound from early caregiving experiences. Through guided dialogue with these parts, healing becomes possible.

2. Somatic Experiencing (SE)

Developed by Peter Levine, SE focuses on releasing trauma stored in the body. Disorganized individuals often feel emotional overwhelm as physical symptoms: tightness in the chest, racing heart, numbness. SE helps them track and release these responses, increasing their capacity to stay present during relational discomfort.

3. EMDR (Eye Movement Desensitization and Reprocessing)

EMDR is effective for processing attachment trauma, particularly when linked to early neglect or abuse. It helps individuals reprocess painful memories and reduce their emotional charge, decreasing reactivity in current relationships.

4. Emotionally Focused Therapy (EFT)

Particularly helpful in couples or family settings, EFT supports safe emotional expression and helps individuals identify triggers rooted in attachment injuries. It enables the disorganized partner to understand that their fear doesn't need to translate into emotional shutdown or aggression.

5. Polyvagal-Informed Therapy

Using Dr. Stephen Porges' polyvagal theory, this approach explains how the nervous system reacts to perceived threats in relationships. Therapists help clients move from states of shutdown (dorsal vagal) to safety and connection (ventral vagal) through breathwork, grounding, and co-regulation.

Practical Tools for Healing

1. Self-Awareness Journaling Prompts

- What triggers your urge to pull away from closeness?

- What part of you is afraid of being known?

- When do you feel safe in relationships? What conditions make that possible?

- How does your body signal when you're moving toward emotional overwhelm?

- What would it feel like to trust that someone could handle all parts of you?

2. Co-Regulation Exercises

Practice grounding with a partner or trusted friend:

- Sit back-to-back and match breathing for 5 minutes

- Hold hands and focus on sensation for 60 seconds

- Use mirroring exercises: one person moves slowly, the other follows

- Practice maintaining eye contact during moments of vulnerability

- Share physical space while doing separate, calming activities

3. Visualization Practices

Create internal safety through guided imagery:

- Visualize a calm place where all parts of you are welcome

- Imagine your "younger self" being comforted by a secure caregiver

- Practice seeing yourself as worthy of consistent, gentle love

- Envision relationships where conflict doesn't mean abandonment

4. Relationship Check-In Tool

Adapted specifically for disorganized attachment:

- Weekly 10-minute check-in with a partner or friend

- Share one fear, one success, and one intention for the coming week

- Practice naming emotions as they arise without judgment

- End with an affirmation like: "Even when it's hard, I choose connection"

Chapter Six

Attachment Style Assessment

"I think I'm all four styles," Maya laughs during her therapy session. "Monday I'm anxious, Tuesday I'm avoidant, Wednesday I'm completely disorganized, and Thursday I feel secure. Am I doing this wrong?"

Her confusion reflects a common misconception: attachment styles aren't rigid categories but dynamic patterns that can shift based on context, stress levels, and relationship dynamics (Fraley, 2019). Understanding your attachment style involves recognizing your dominant patterns while acknowledging the complexity of human relationships.

The Reality of Attachment Styles

Primary vs. Secondary Patterns

Most people have a primary attachment style—their default pattern under normal circumstances—along with secondary tendencies that emerge during stress or with specific types of relationships (Simpson & Rholes, 2017).

Example: Sarah is generally secure in her friendships and family relationships but becomes anxious in romantic contexts due to past relationship trauma. Her primary style is secure, but romantic attachment triggers her secondary anxious patterns.

Another example: Marcus maintains avoidant patterns with his family of origin but has developed secure attachment with his chosen family of close friends. Context and relationship history shape which patterns emerge.

Contextual Triggers

Different situations can activate different attachment responses:

High stress periods: Even securely attached individuals may show anxious or avoidant behaviors during major life transitions, health crises, or work pressures

Relationship stages: Some people feel secure during dating but anxious as relationships deepen, or comfortable with friendship but avoidant of romantic intimacy

Partner influence: Your attachment style can be influenced by your partner's style—anxious partners may activate avoidant responses, while secure partners often help regulate insecure patterns

Comprehensive Attachment Assessment

Self-Reflection Questions

Relationship History Patterns:

    1. What themes repeat across your significant relationships?

2. How do your relationships typically begin? How do they usually end?

3. What relationship conflicts feel most threatening to you?

4. When do you feel most and least secure in relationships?

5. How do you typically respond when partners need space? When they seek closeness?

Emotional Response Patterns:

1. How do you typically handle your own distress? Do you seek support or manage alone?

2. What happens in your body when relationships feel uncertain?

3. How comfortable are you expressing emotions directly?

4. How do you respond when others express strong emotions?

5. What triggers your strongest relationship fears?

Communication and Conflict Patterns:

1. How do you typically handle relationship disagreements?

2. Do you tend to pursue resolution or need space during conflicts?

3. How direct are you about expressing needs and boundaries?

4. What happens when others are direct with you about their needs?

The Attachment Style Spectrum Assessment

Rate each statement from 1 (never true) to 5 (always true):

Secure Indicators:

- I feel comfortable depending on others and having them depend on me (____/5)

- I can express my needs directly without fear of rejection (____/5)

- I handle relationship conflicts with curiosity rather than defensiveness (____/5)

- I maintain my sense of self while being emotionally available to others (____/5)

- I trust that relationships can weather difficulties and grow stronger (____/5)

Anxious Indicators:

- I worry frequently about being abandoned or rejected (____/5)

- I need regular reassurance to feel secure in relationships (____/5)

- I often feel like I care more about the relationship than my partner does (____/5)

- Small changes in my partner's behavior trigger significant anxiety (____/5)

- I have difficulty enjoying time alone without thinking about my relationships (_____/5)

Avoidant Indicators:

- I value my independence above almost everything else in relationships (_____/5)

- I feel uncomfortable when people try to get very close emotionally (_____/5)

- I prefer to handle problems on my own rather than seeking support (_____/5)

- I tend to withdraw when relationships become emotionally intense (_____/5)

- I find it difficult to depend on others, even when I need help (_____/5)

Disorganized Indicators:

- I feel torn between wanting closeness and fearing it (_____/5)

- My emotions in relationships feel intense and difficult to control (_____/5)

- I sometimes act in ways that push people away when I most want them close (_____/5)

- I have difficulty trusting others, even when they've been consistently reliable (_____/5)

- My relationship behaviors sometimes feel contradictory or confusing to others (_____/5)

Interpreting Your Scores:

- **Highest scoring category:** Likely your primary attachment style

- **Second-highest:** Your secondary tendencies or stress responses

- **Similar scores across categories:** Suggests more situational/contextual attachment patterns

- **High scores in multiple insecure categories:** May indicate disorganized attachment or complex trauma history

Understanding Your Attachment Through Relationships

Romantic Relationship Patterns

Early relationship stages:

- **Secure:** Comfortable pace, authentic self-presentation, realistic expectations

- **Anxious:** Intense connection, fantasy about future, high investment quickly

- **Avoidant:** Careful pace, emphasis on compatibility and independence, emotional walls

- **Disorganized:** Chaotic intensity, simultaneous attraction and fear, push-pull dynamics

During conflict:

- **Secure:** Curiosity about partner's perspective, focus on resolution, emotional regulation

- **Anxious:** Fear that conflict threatens the relationship, pursuit of immediate resolution, emotional flooding

- **Avoidant:** Discomfort with emotional expression, preference for space and time, logical focus

- **Disorganized:** Overwhelming emotional responses, fight-or-flight activation, contradictory behaviors

With commitment:

- **Secure:** Natural progression based on compatibility and growth

- **Anxious:** Relief and anxiety—wanting commitment but fearing it won't last

- **Avoidant:** Anxiety about loss of independence, carefully negotiated terms

- **Disorganized:** Simultaneous craving and terror, sabotage behaviors, internal conflict

Family Relationship Indicators

With parents/family of origin:

- How do you feel when visiting family?

- What role do you typically play in family dynamics?

- How do you handle family conflict or drama?

- Do you seek family support during difficulties?

Example patterns:

- **Secure:** Maintains healthy boundaries while staying connected, can disagree without cutting off relationship

- **Anxious:** May become enmeshed in family drama, seeks approval, difficulty setting boundaries

- **Avoidant:** Maintains surface-level relationships, avoids family emotional intensity, self-reliant during crises

- **Disorganized:** Conflicted family relationships, alternates between closeness and distance, complicated loyalty patterns

Friendship Patterns

Making friends:

- **Secure:** Natural social connections, appropriate pace of intimacy development

- **Anxious:** Intense new friendships, may over-share quickly, needs frequent contact

- **Avoidant:** Slower to develop close friendships, prefers activity-based connections

- **Disorganized:** Chaotic friendship patterns, difficulty maintaining consistent connections

Maintaining friendships:

- **Secure:** Consistent contact, mutual support, healthy

boundaries

- **Anxious:** High maintenance friendships, may pursue friends who withdraw

- **Avoidant:** Loyal but independent, shows care through actions rather than words

- **Disorganized:** On-and-off friendships, misunderstandings, difficulty with trust

Cultural and Familial Influences on Attachment

Cultural Attachment Norms

Different cultures express attachment in varying ways that may not fit Western psychological categories (Keller, 2018):

Collectivist cultures: May emphasize interdependence in ways that appear "anxious" but represent healthy cultural norms

Cultures valuing emotional restraint: May appear "avoidant" but maintain deep connections through action and presence

Cultures with different family structures: Extended family systems may create secure attachment through multiple caregivers

Example: In Mei-Lin's Chinese family, emotional restraint and family

Chapter Seven

Setting Healthy Boundaries

C ompassion while maintaining boundaries can look like anything: occasionally going out of your way for the people you love without regularly over giving to the point where you feel exhausted, recognizing that relationships aren't always 50/50, and caring about your partner's opinion without letting it overshadow the essential decisions you have to make. These delicate balances shape the architecture of healthy relationships.

Boundaries exist as acts of love—both for yourself and others. Think of them as the banks of a river, containing its flow while allowing its strength. Without them, love can flood, overwhelming both the giver and the receiver. It is too rigid, and the connection struggles to flow at all. The trick is to find a spot where care and limits dance together, where yes and no can live in the same space, and where giving feels sustainable rather than depleting.

Most of us learn about boundaries hard—through burnout, resentment, or relationships where we lose ourselves trying to be everything for someone else. But in these lessons, there's also empowerment. We realize that constantly saying yes eventually turns into unspoken no's, and being available to everyone often leaves us unable to be fully present for anyone. That love without limits frequently transforms into limitation without love. Setting boundaries is not a sign of weakness, but a powerful act of self-preservation and self-respect.

This chapter explores drawing lines that protect while staying soft enough to connect.

Why Boundaries Matter

Rivers can hold a great deal, but just because their capacity to carry is great does not mean they should contain everything poured into them.

The same applies to people, especially the ones with big hearts and a natural inclination to nurture. Your capacity to care, give, and understand others might feel endless. Still, without boundaries, even the deepest wells run dry.

Boundaries protect us from the subtle erosion of self that happens when we consistently override our limits. Prioritizing others' needs at your expense causes resentment, exhaustion, and lost dreams—this is not deep love.

Setting boundaries signals something profound to yourself and others: that your needs matter as much as theirs, that love can exist alongside limits, and that respect flows both ways. Think of the partner who learns to say, "I need a few minutes to myself after work," instead of immediately diving into household demands, or the friend who kindly declines a favor because their plate is full. These small acts of self-respect ripple outward, creating relationships built on mutual understanding rather than obligation or resentment.

Boundaries as Self-Care

Self-care is learning to notice the space between your cup is overflowing and completely dry. Most people understand self-care through external actions, such as bubble baths, meditation apps, and weekend getaways. But proper self-care often involves saying no when you mean no, protecting your peace even when others push back, and staying committed to your well-being even when it feels uncomfortable.

The magic happens in small daily choices: blocking off quiet time in your morning routine, turning your phone off during dinner, and letting calls go to voicemail when you need focus time. These aren't acts of selfishness but moments of self-preservation that allow you to show up more fully in your relationships.

The practice starts with tuning into your signals, noticing when your shoulders tense during certain conversations when your energy dips after specific interactions, and when your joy feels dimmed by obligations. These physical and emotional cues indicate where boundaries need to be strengthened, clearly highlighting areas that require shoring up your emotional defenses.

Steps to Define Personal Limits

To muster up the courage to call upon the vocabulary that'll help you express your limits—these feel like impossible tasks when you've spent years being someone else's container. The words stick in your throat, feelings tangle with fear, and that voice in your head whispers, "Maybe I'm asking for too much." Setting boundaries can sometimes feel like learning a new language, where your needs deserve just as much space as everyone else's.

Expressing boundaries starts somewhere between whispered "maybes" and confident "nos." It is between knowing what you need and finding the strength to voice it, between understanding your limits and believing you deserve to enforce them. Expressing your boundaries isn't about building impenetrable walls or pushing people away—it's about creating clear channels where respect can flow both ways.

Setting boundaries, protecting your energy, and stating your needs honors yourself while connecting with others. These moments add up, creating patterns of self-respect that reshape how you engage in all your relationships.

Self-Reflection

Knowing what boundaries you need to enforce or what your needs are will require you to look inward with radical honesty. Most of us respond to others' needs, adapt to their preferences, and shift our shapes to fit their expectations.

Self-reflection asks us to pause this constant adaptation and take stock of where we stand.

Start with questions that reveal your edges:

- When do you feel resentful in relationships?

- Where do you consistently override your own needs?

- What situations leave you feeling depleted rather than fulfilled?

- What triggers your emotional flooding?

- Which relationships require a "recovery period" after interaction?

- What parts of yourself do you hide to keep peace?

Take inventory of your body's wisdom—moments when your stomach tightens, sleep becomes restless, and joy dims. Your physical responses often recognize boundary violations before your mind catches up. Notice patterns: which relationships drain you, which commitments leave you feeling hollow, which requests make you want to hide.

Pay attention to your delayed reactions, too—the conversations you replay in your mind hours later. These situations leave you slightly off. Still, you can't explain why, the commitments you regret making as soon as you're alone. These delayed responses often point to boundaries you need but haven't yet learned to voice.

Identifying Values and Needs

Our values and needs teach us what we must protect in relationships. They act as internal guides, showing us where to draw lines and when to stand firm. If you value authenticity, you might be more inclined to set boundaries around pretending to be okay when they're not. If you cherish deep connections, you should limit superficial social obligations that drain energy from meaningful relationships.

Consider your non-negotiables—those core values that make you who you are:

- What qualities do you most admire in others?

- Which moments in life have felt most aligned with your truth?

- When do you feel most proud of how you've shown up?

- What do you want people to remember about how you treated them?

- What principles would you defend even if it cost you something?

These answers reveal what needs protection through clear boundaries:

- Space for solitude and reflection.

- Freedom to express authentic feelings.

- Time for personal growth and learning.

- Room to change your mind without guilt.

- Permission to prioritize your well-being.

- Ability to say no without endless explanation.

Understanding your values helps transform boundary-setting from a defensive act into an affirmative one. Instead of building walls to keep others out, you're creating sacred space for what matters most to flourish.

Communicating Your Boundaries

The communication aspect of boundary setting might be one of the most challenging aspects of everything. How do you communicate your point without sounding like you're pushing people away?

How do you say, "I need space," without making others feel rejected? How do you express limits without coming across as complex or demanding?

These questions often keep us silent when we most need to speak.

We may learn early on in life that setting boundaries means connection and that asking for what we need might lead to losing what we have. So, we stopped saying no and started saying maybe. We may pad our limits with apologies and wrap our boundaries in so many explanations that they lose their power. We end up saying everything except what we mean.

The challenge is to find words that honor our needs and relationships—words that convey kindness without cruelty, firmness without defensiveness, respect for ourselves, and care for others. When communicated clearly, boundaries don't damage connections; they create the conditions for real intimacy to flourish.

Be Kind, Not Cruel

Kindness in boundary setting means choosing words that honor your needs and the other person's dignity. Instead of "You're always dumping your problems on me," try "I care about what you're going through, and I also need to preserve my own emotional energy." This approach maintains connection while establishing limits. Remember: You can be kind and firm—they're not mutually exclusive.

Be Direct and Assertive

Dancing around boundaries with hints and hopes rarely works. The precise language leaves no room for misunderstanding. Replace "Maybe we could possibly..." with "I need..." or "This doesn't work for me." Let your yes be yes and your no be no. Skip the lengthy explanations and justifications—you don't need to defend your right to have limits.

Be Aware of Power Dynamics

Different relationships require different approaches. Setting boundaries with a boss feels different from setting them with a friend. With authority figures, frame boundaries regarding what will help you perform better. In close relationships, focus on how boundaries will strengthen your connection. With people who tend to push limits, be prepared to restate your position calmly.

Practice What You Want to Say

Meaningful conversations deserve rehearsal. First, try writing down your boundaries on paper. It will help clarify your thoughts. Then, practice in front of a mirror or with a trusted friend. Notice where you start to apologize or overexplain. Pay attention to your body language; your nonverbal cues should match your words.

Maintaining Respect and Balance

Maya and her mother shared what she calls "the Sunday night ritual." Those weekly phone calls would last hours as her mother detailed every family drama, neighborhood scandal, and personal grievance she'd collected over the week. Maya would sit there, her phone pressed to her ear, feeling her evening slip away and her Monday anxiety build. "I love my mom," she explains, "but those calls were draining me. I needed to change something without damaging our relationship."

The solution gradually emerged, and Maya learned to say, "Mom, I can give you my full attention for thirty minutes, and then I need to prep for my week." Her mother initially resisted, but Maya stayed consistent—warm but firm. Now, their calls feel meaningful rather than marathons. "The funny thing is," Maya notes, "our conversations got better. When I respected my own limits, our relationship actually deepened."

Their story highlights something crucial about boundary maintenance: it's not about building walls but about creating sustainable connections. When we learn to hold both respect for others and respect for ourselves on the same hand, relationships have room to find their natural, healthy rhythm; this is how you can achieve those healthy rhythms:

Like training a muscle, boundaries grow stronger through consistent use. When you say you need time after work to decompress, honor that time, even on good days. When you set limits around lending money, maintain them regardless of who's asking. Wavering boundaries invite testing, while consistent ones earn respect. Each time you uphold a boundary, you reinforce its importance to others and yourself.

When boundaries get crossed, your response sets the tone for future interactions. Stay calm but clear: "We agreed on thirty minutes for coffee, and I need to leave now," rather than making excuses or getting defensive. Address violations promptly rather than letting resentment build. Remember that people often test boundaries not from malice but from habit. Your consistent, respectful reinforcement helps them learn new patterns.

Creating a balanced dynamic: Balance emerges from mutual respect for your boundaries and others'. When someone expresses their limits, honor them as you want yours honored.

Evaluate relationship dynamics: Notice when relationships feel lopsided in either direction. Are you always the giver or always the receiver? Do boundaries flow both ways? Healthy relationships include space for people's needs, limits, and growth.

Repeat this (as many times as you may need to):

- I value relationships built on honesty, vulnerability, and connection, so I must show up and practice those things, even when it's scary.

- I value people who can say no without needing to explain themselves, who respect my boundaries even when they don't understand them, who express their needs clearly and directly, who take responsibility for their own emotions, who stay present during difficult conversations, and who honor both connection and independence.

- I prioritize self-care, kindness, and open communication.

These aren't just statements—they're promises to yourself. Write them down. Speak them aloud. Let them remind you that boundaries aren't acts of distance but declarations of self-respect. Each time you honor them, you teach others how to love you better while learning to love yourself more deeply.

Chapter Eight

Attachment Styles in the Workplace

T he conference room falls silent as Sarah delivers her quarterly presentation. While her data is solid and her insights valuable, her colleagues notice the subtle signs: how she checks her phone between slides for reassuring messages, the way her voice wavers when discussing potential challenges, and her need to circle back repeatedly to ensure everyone agrees with her conclusions. Meanwhile, across the hall, David runs his team meetings with military precision—agenda items timed to the minute, emotions kept carefully in check, and any attempts at personal connection redirected back to business metrics.

These aren't just different management styles or personality quirks. They're attachment patterns in professional dress, revealing how our earliest relationship blueprints shape every aspect of our working lives. The same neural pathways that learned to navigate love and safety in childhood now orchestrate our responses to authority, collaboration, conflict, and professional intimacy.

Understanding attachment in the workplace isn't just an academic exercise—it's a practical necessity in today's relationship-driven economy. Research by the Harvard Business Review shows that emotional intelligence accounts for 58% of job performance across all industries (Bradberry & Greaves, 2009). Yet most professionals remain unaware of how their attachment patterns influence their leadership effectiveness, team dynamics, and career trajectories.

The Hidden Architecture of Professional Behavior

Our attachment styles create invisible blueprints that shape how we navigate the complex social ecosystem of modern workplaces. These patterns influence everything from how we respond to supervision to our comfort with networking, from our approach to workplace conflict to our capacity for professional vulnerability.

Consider how attachment manifests in daily workplace interactions. The anxiously attached employee who sends follow-up emails within minutes of meetings isn't just being thorough—their nervous system is seeking reassurance that professional relationships remain secure. The avoidant manager who communicates primarily through formal channels isn't being cold—they're maintaining the emotional distance that feels safest for sustained professional relationships.

Research by Hazan and Shaver (1990) found that attachment styles significantly influence career choices, work satisfaction, and professional relationship quality. Their landmark study revealed that securely attached individuals were more likely to choose careers involving interpersonal contact, while avoidantly attached individuals gravitated toward independent, task-focused roles. These patterns continue to shape workplace dynamics decades later.

Leadership Through an Attachment Lens

Leadership effectiveness correlates strongly with attachment security, though each style brings both strengths and challenges to management roles. Understanding these patterns helps explain why some leaders inspire loyalty while others create anxiety, why some teams thrive under pressure while others fragment, and why certain organizational cultures promote psychological safety while others breed fear and competition.

The Anxious Leader: Passionate but Overwhelming

Anxiously attached leaders bring extraordinary dedication and emotional investment to their roles. They care deeply about their teams' success and well-being, often going above and beyond to support individual growth and project outcomes. Their sensitivity to interpersonal dynamics makes them skilled at reading team morale and identifying relationship issues before they escalate.

However, their fear of failure and need for reassurance can create challenging dynamics. Research by Simpson et al. (2007) demonstrates that anxiously attached individuals show heightened sensitivity to negative feedback, which can translate into micromanagement behaviors as leaders seek to control outcomes and prevent criticism.

Anxious leaders typically:

- Monitor team performance obsessively, interpreting minor setbacks as major threats

- Seek frequent validation from supervisors, peers, and subordinates

- Struggle with delegation due to fears that others won't meet their standards

- Take team failures personally, often assuming responsibility for others' mistakes

- Create dependency relationships where team members feel pressure to provide reassurance

*Case Study: Maria, VP of Marketing*Maria built her reputation on her team's exceptional performance and her dedication to professional development. However, her leadership style created exhaustion among her direct reports. She scheduled daily check-ins that felt like interrogations, sent follow-up emails late into the evening, and became visibly distressed when projects faced normal setbacks. Her team described feeling constantly watched and evaluated, leading to decreased creativity and increased turnover.

The transformation came when Maria recognized her attachment patterns and began implementing structured boundaries. She limited check-ins to twice weekly, established "communication windows" to prevent after-hours emails, and practiced sitting with uncertainty rather than immediately seeking reassurance. Her team's performance improved dramatically as psychological safety increased.

The Avoidant Leader: Competent but Distant

Avoidantly attached leaders excel at strategic thinking, decision-making under pressure, and maintaining organizational focus during turbulent times. Their emotional stability and independence make them natural crisis managers, able to make difficult decisions without being overwhelmed by interpersonal concerns.

Their challenge lies in building the emotional connections that inspire loyalty and engagement. Research by Mayseless (2010) shows that avoidant leaders often struggle with employee retention and team cohesion, as their emotional distance can leave team members feeling undervalued and disconnected.

Avoidant leaders typically:

- Maintain professional boundaries that feel rigid or impersonal

- Focus on tasks and metrics while missing emotional undercurrents

- Avoid team-building activities or informal relationship development

- Struggle to provide emotional support during difficult periods

- Make decisions unilaterally without soliciting input or buy-in

*Case Study: James, Director of Operations*James ran his department with impressive efficiency. Projects completed on time, budgets stayed within limits, and quality metrics consistently exceeded targets. Yet his annual employee satisfaction scores were consistently low, with comments like "feels like working for a robot" and "doesn't seem to care about us as people."

The shift began when James participated in 360-degree feedback and recognized how his emotional distance affected team dynamics. He implemented weekly "coffee talks" with no agenda beyond relationship building, began acknowledging personal milestones like birthdays and work anniversaries, and practiced asking about team members' perspectives before making decisions. While maintaining his natural preference for professional boundaries, he learned to create moments of authentic connection that dramatically improved team morale and retention.

The Secure Leader: The Gold Standard

Securely attached leaders create the psychological safety that enables high performance, innovation, and resilience. They balance support with autonomy, provide clear expectations while remaining flexible, and handle conflict as an opportunity for growth rather than a threat to stability.

Research by Khoury et al. (2018) demonstrates that teams led by securely attached managers show higher levels of creativity, job satisfaction, and organizational commitment. These leaders create environments where employees feel safe to take risks, admit mistakes, and engage in the kind of vulnerable conversations that drive breakthrough results.

Secure leaders typically:

- Provide consistent, reliable support while encouraging independence

- Handle conflict with curiosity rather than defensiveness

- Balance emotional attunement with clear professional boundaries

- Adapt their leadership style to individual team members' needs

- Model vulnerability and authentic communication

The Disorganized Leader: Chaos in the Corner Office

Disorganized attachment in leadership creates unpredictable organizational climates where team members never know which version of their leader they'll encounter. These leaders may alternate between over-involvement and complete withdrawal, creating confusion and anxiety throughout their teams.

However, when stabilized through therapy or coaching, formerly disorganized leaders often bring remarkable creativity, adaptability, and emotional intelligence to their roles. Their lived experience with complexity can translate into sophisticated understanding of organizational dynamics and change management.

Disorganized leaders typically:

- Create unpredictable team dynamics through inconsistent behavior

- Struggle with emotional regulation during high-stress periods

- Send mixed messages about expectations and priorities

- Have difficulty maintaining professional boundaries consistently

- May excel during crisis situations but struggle with routine management

Team Dynamics and Collaboration Patterns

The interaction between different attachment styles creates predictable team dynamics that can either enhance or derail collaborative efforts. Understanding these patterns helps explain why some teams gel immediately while others struggle with seemingly simple projects, why certain combinations of personalities create friction, and how to optimize team composition for specific outcomes.

The Anxious-Avoidant Workplace Dance

One of the most common and challenging workplace dynamics occurs when anxiously attached employees work closely with avoidant colleagues or supervisors. This creates a pursuit-distance cycle that can paralyze productivity and poison team relationships.

The anxiously attached team member interprets their avoidant colleague's independence as rejection or disengagement, leading to increased efforts to connect—more emails, more meeting requests, more attempts at relationship building. The avoidant colleague, feeling overwhelmed by this intensity, withdraws further, creating a negative feedback loop that can escalate to workplace conflicts or formal complaints.

*Example: The Marketing-Engineering Interface*At a tech startup, the marketing team (predominantly anxious attachment) consistently clashed with the engineering team (predominantly avoidant attachment). Marketing's requests for frequent updates and collaborative sessions were met with engineering's preference for written communication and minimal meetings. The conflict escalated when marketing interpreted engineering's communication style as arrogance and lack of cooperation, while engineering viewed marketing as needy and disorganized.

Resolution came through attachment-aware team building that helped each group understand the other's communication preferences and work styles. Marketing learned to batch their requests and provide more structured interaction opportunities, while engineering committed to more frequent but time-limited check-ins and clearer status communication.

Cross-Functional Collaboration Challenges

Different attachment styles naturally gravitate toward certain functions and roles, creating predictable friction points in cross-functional collaboration:

Sales and Marketing (often anxious-leaning): Focus on relationships, frequent communication, emotional connection with customers and colleagues

Finance and Operations (often avoidant-leaning): Emphasis on systems, processes, data-driven decisions, minimal interpersonal complexity

Human Resources and Customer Service (often secure-leaning): Balance of relationship focus and systematic approach, natural mediators

Creative and Strategy roles (mixed attachment styles): Can include disorganized attachment patterns that bring innovation but may struggle with implementation

Understanding these patterns helps organizations design better collaboration protocols, communication strategies, and conflict resolution processes that honor different attachment needs while achieving business objectives.

Performance Management and Career Development

Attachment styles significantly influence how employees respond to performance feedback, career coaching, and professional development opportunities. Traditional performance management approaches often fail because they don't account for these fundamental differences in how people process feedback and navigate professional relationships.

Chapter Nine

Applying Theory Across Workplace

A ttachment styles are not confined to romantic relationships. They are the fabric of our human connections, playing out in every corner of our lives. Spend an hour in a coffee shop and witness these patterns in action. The manager who dictates every detail at work most likely does the same in her personal life. The barista who over-apologizes to customers may likely handle her friendships with a similar level of caution. And the customer who keeps everyone at arm's length? He's maintaining the same careful distance in all his relationships.

Our attachment style, a universal blueprint for human connection, extends beyond romance.

These patterns weave through every relationship we form, from the brief interaction with a grocery clerk to the decade-long friend-ships. An anxious colleague who needs constant reassurance about their work performance may often double-text their dates, too. The avoidant friend who disappears during emotional conversations will surely maintain the same careful distance from their family. The securely attached mentor who sets clear, kind boundaries with students will navigate their relationships with similar grace.

Understanding how attachment styles shape our connections is a key to unlocking deeper self-awareness. It explains why certain professional relationships can trigger issues, some friendships can drain us, and family dynamics can stir up old wounds. This understanding provides insight and paves the way for personal growth and healing.

More importantly, it shows us where healing in one area of life can create positive ripples through all our relationships.

Attachment in Digital Relationships and Social Media

Our online lives have changed how we connect, but not why we connect. Social media and digital communication platforms often amplify attachment tendencies, creating new arenas where our deepest relationship patterns play out in real time. The same fears of abandonment, needs for control, and desires for an authentic connection that shape our face-to-face relationships now manifest through screens, notifications, and digital interactions.

Anxious Attachment Online:

Individuals with anxious attachment often find themselves trapped in cycles of digital vigilance, frequently checking messages and social media for validation through likes, comments, and responses. They experience heightened sensitivity to being "left on read" or receiving delayed replies, with each message with no reply triggering waves of anxiety and self-doubt. The nature of social media becomes particularly triggering as we may compare ourselves to others. When someone is "active" online but hasn't responded, then anxiety can spike as they imagine worst-case scenarios. They over-analyze every aspect of digital communication—timing, tone, frequency, and even punctuation—searching for signs of approval or rejection in each interaction.

Sarah consistently checks social media for signs of connection and acceptance, experiencing anxiety when she feels excluded. The digital world becomes a 24/7 source of potential rejection signals, transforming what should be connection tools into instruments of emotional torment.

Avoidant Attachment Online:

Individuals with avoidant attachment maintain their characteristic emotional distance even in digital spaces, often ignoring messages for extended periods to control the pace and intensity of relationships. They prefer one-way content consumption over interactive engagement, scrolling through feeds without commenting or reacting, especially when posts contain emotional vulnerability or personal sharing. When they receive messages, they frequently read them but deliberately delay responding, sometimes for days, as immediate replies feel too intimate or demanding. They gravitate toward text-based communication over video calls, finding the latter too emotionally exposing and preferring the safety of written words where they can carefully control their presentation. They maintain a distant social media presence, sharing mostly neutral content.

Mark keeps his read receipts off, takes days to respond to even close friends, and scrolls through emotional posts without engaging. He consumes content but rarely contributes anything personal, maintaining his characteristic distance even in digital spaces where connection feels safer yet somehow more threatening than ever.

Disorganized Attachment Online:

Individuals with disorganized attachment bring their internal chaos into digital spaces, creating erratic online behaviors that reflect their push-pull relationship with intimacy. Fear of exposure leads to deleting vulnerable late-night posts. This creates a pattern of seeking closeness through social media while simultaneously fearing the real-world intimacy that might result from their digital vulnerability. They cycle between over sharing and complete digital withdrawal. Their online presence often includes creating drama through cryptic posts or indirect communication, posting vague messages that hint at distress without revealing specifics, forcing others to guess at their needs. Despite being constantly connected through various platforms, they feel simultaneously engaged and profoundly isolated, as digital interactions provide a semblance of connection while maintaining enough distance to avoid true intimacy.

Emma posts vulnerable content late at night, then deletes it by morning, craving the connection that comes from online validation while fearing the intimacy that might follow. Her digital behavior creates cycles of reach and retreat that mirror her offline relationships, leaving her followers confused and her own needs perpetually unmet.

Secure Attachment Online:

Individuals with secure attachment bring their emotional stability and relationship confidence into digital spaces, engaging in balanced online behaviors that reflect their comfort with both connection and independence. They maintain healthy engagement patterns without compulsive checking of messages or social media, responding to communications when convenient rather than feeling pressured to reply immediately. Their digital communication is clear, direct, and respectful, avoiding the passive-aggressive undertones or desperate seeking behaviors common in other attachment styles. They feel comfortable with occasional digital distance, understanding that delayed responses or periods of reduced contact don't signal relationship threats or personal rejection. When they share personal content, it comes from a place of authentic expression rather than validation-seeking, and they're able to post without anxiously monitoring likes, comments, or reactions. Most importantly, they maintain healthy boundaries around screen time and availability, recognizing that constant digital connection isn't necessary for maintaining secure relationships.

Creating Healthier Digital Attachment Patterns:

Developing more secure digital behaviors starts with setting intentional boundaries around screen time and message response expectations, recognizing that immediate availability isn't a relationship requirement. It's helpful to unfollow accounts that consistently trigger feelings of insecurity, inadequacy, or unhealthy comparison, curating your digital environment to support rather than undermine your well-being. Communicating openly with close contacts about your communication style can prevent misunderstandings—letting friends know delayed responses aren't personal rejections helps reduce attachment-related anxiety on both sides. Learning to sit with the discomfort of delayed responses, whether giving or receiving them, builds tolerance for the natural ebb and flow of digital communication. The goal is using technology to enhance rather than replace face-to-face connections, treating digital interactions as supplements to, not substitutes for, real-world intimacy. Addressing attachment fears from digital interactions directly, rather than impulsively reacting, helps build healthier online relationships.

Attachment Styles in the Workplace

The same patterns that shape our relationships quietly orchestrate our professional lives. That colleague who insists on controlling every project detail, avoids delegating, and keeps her office door firmly shut? She's likely carrying her avoidant attachment style into the workplace. Then there's the teammate who constantly craves feedback, panics when emails go unanswered and takes every bit of criticism to heart—that's anxious attachment, dressed in business casual.

Leadership styles often mirror attachment patterns:

- The anxious leader micromanages because of fear of losing control.

- The avoidant boss maintains emotional distance through pure professionalism.

- The secure manager balances support with independence.

- The disorganized leader swings between over-involvement and complete detachment.

These patterns show up most clearly in how people handle common workplace scenarios:

Team Projects: The avoidant colleague prefers working alone, bristling at group meetings and collaborative requirements. The anxiously attached team member constantly checks in, needing reassurance that their work meets expectations. The secure colleague maintains healthy communication while respecting others' autonomy.

Feedback Sessions: Anxious employees might struggle to hear constructive criticism without taking it personally, while avoidant ones might dismiss important feedback entirely. Secure workers tend to receive feedback with openness, seeing it as an opportunity for growth rather than a threat to their worth.

Attachment and Leadership in the Workplace

Attachment patterns profoundly influence how we lead, follow, collaborate, and manage conflict at work. Understanding these patterns can transform workplace dynamics and create more effective, emotionally intelligent leadership.

Secure Leaders inspire trust through consistent, reliable behavior and create psychologically safe environments where team members feel valued. They give constructive feedback without triggering shame, model vulnerability by admitting mistakes publicly, and balance support with autonomy, knowing when to intervene and when to step back. Their leadership style fosters openness and resilience throughout their teams.

Anxious-Attached Leaders often seek constant reassurance from staff or micromanage because of fear of failure, struggling with delegation because they fear losing control or that others won't meet their standards. They may overreact to perceived rejection or feedback from superiors and team members, becoming overwhelmed by interpersonal conflicts and team dynamics that trigger their attachment insecurities.

Avoidant-Attached Leaders appear aloof or overly self-reliant, struggling to connect emotionally with team members while focusing heavily on tasks and outcomes at the expense of relational leadership. They avoid tough conversations about performance or team dynamics and may cannot provide the emotional support their team needs during challenging periods.

Disorganized-Attached Leaders create confusion by alternating between closeness and distance, struggling with emotional consistency under stress and creating unpredictable work environments.

They often have difficulty maintaining clear boundaries between personal and professional relationships, leaving team members uncertain about expectations and dynamics.

Developing attachment-aware leadership by reflecting on your style and actively listening to team needs. Strong leaders provide consistent feedback, model fixing mistakes, and communicate clearly, adapting to team needs.

Family Interactions and Dynamics

When you think about your childhood, specific memories stand out like photographs. It may be how your mother's face would tighten when you asked for emotional support or how your father could fill a room with silence when he felt overwhelmed.

Perhaps you remember learning early that big feelings weren't welcome at the dinner table or that neediness would be met with distance. These weren't just moments—they were lessons in attachment that now shape how you move through your family relationships.

Family systems operate like emotional ecosystems where attachment patterns pass through generations, like inherited traits. Watch any family gathering, and you'll see the dance: the aunt who keeps everyone at bay while complaining no one visits. Or the sister who constantly texts when anyone travels, and the brother who disappears during emotional conversations, only to resurface when things feel lighter. These aren't just personality quirks—they're attachment adaptations playing out in real time.

Understanding these patterns offers hope. It allows us to see family dynamics not as fixed traits but as learned responses that, with awareness and intention, can shift toward more secure connections.

Parent-Child Attachment

Parent-child relationships act as mirrors, reflecting attachment patterns with startling clarity. The anxiously attached mother might check her teenager's location app too frequently, her fear of abandonment masquerading as concern for safety. The avoidant father might struggle with his toddler's emotional needs, unconsciously recreating the emotional distance he experienced in his own childhood.

Everyday responses reveal these patterns in our emotional reactions to our children's big feelings. Our physical presence shows in how we respond to requests for attention, our comfort with affection, and our ability to balance independence with protection while reading non-verbal cues. Openness about feelings, conflict resolution, curiosity, and admitting mistakes shape communication.

The brain's neuroplasticity offers hope—our capacity to create new patterns means change is possible. Each conscious choice to respond differently, each moment we choose connection over reactive patterns, rewrites our attachment story and shapes our children's future relationships. Breaking intergenerational cycles happens one mindful response at a time, transforming both our parenting and our children's developing sense of security in relationships.

Parenting for Secure Attachment

Secure attachment doesn't require perfection—it requires consistency, responsiveness, and emotional availability. As a parent, you have the power to shape your child's attachment style, and with the right practices, you can foster a secure and healthy relationship.

Good parenting isn't about being perfect. It's about meeting your child's needs, fixing mistakes when they happen, and giving them a secure base to explore from.

Key Practices for Parents include tuning in by noticing and responding to your child's cues for comfort, attention, or space, while reflecting their feelings by naming emotions as they arise, such as saying, "You seem frustrated about your toy not working." When you lose your temper or miss important cues, repair these ruptures by apologizing and reconnecting authentically, showing your child that relationships can survive conflict and mistakes.

Encourage autonomy by letting your child explore independently while knowing you're a safe base they can return to. Additionally, model emotion regulation by demonstrating what calm self-regulation looks like during stressful moments.

These practices create the foundation for secure attachment, teaching children they are worthy of love. And, that relationships are safe spaces for authentic expression, and that they can confidently explore the world knowing they have a reliable source of comfort and support to return to when needed.

Tips by Age Group:

Infants (0-18 months):

- Skin-to-skin contact and responsive caregiving.

- Consistent soothing routines during distress.

- Reading and responding to hunger, sleep, and comfort cues.

- Creating predictable daily rhythms.

Toddlers (18 months-3 years):

- Simple emotion naming: "You're angry the blocks fell down."

- Predictable routines with flexibility for developmental needs.

- Offering age-appropriate choices to foster autonomy.

- Staying calm during tantrums while providing comfort.

Children (3-12 years):

- Validating emotions while setting loving limits on behavior.

- Supporting problem-solving rather than immediately rescuing.

- Creating space for age-appropriate independence.

- Regular one-on-one time for connection and conversation.

Teens (12+ years):

- Respecting growing independence while maintaining connection.

- Open dialogue about challenges without trying to "fix" everything.

- Emotional coaching during difficult life transitions.

- Balancing support with space for identity development.

Remember: It's not about being perfect. It's about being present, attuned, and willing to repair when things go wrong. Children don't need perfect parents—they need authentic, responsive ones who can acknowledge mistakes and work to reconnect.

Siblings and Attachment

Craig and Anna are close, but not the kind of close where they'd call each other about a bad day or share their deeper fears. They maintain what Craig calls "comfortable distance." For him, this comfort includes showing up for holidays, exchanging birthday texts, and keeping conversations safe about work updates and weekend plans. When asked about their relationship, both say it's "fine," with a particular tone that suggests there's more beneath the surface.

Their dynamic tells a familiar story of sibling attachment: two people who share a history but navigate intimacy differently. While Anna yearns for deeper connection, regularly reaching out only to feel rebuffed, Craig maintains his emotional walls with practiced ease. It's something they learned early—Anna, the anxious pursuer. Craig, the avoidant distancer—roles that crystallized in childhood and followed them into adulthood.

What looks like personality differences or simple preferences often reveals deeper attachment patterns. The same strategies siblings developed to handle their parents' emotional availability (or lack thereof) usually shape how they relate. These early blueprints for connection don't just affect individual relationships—they create the emotional temperature of entire family systems.

These patterns show up clearly in how siblings navigate their adult relationships with each other:

Competitive dynamics: Early experiences of competing for parental attention often create lasting patterns. The anxiously attached sibling might still seek validation through achievement or comparison, while the avoidant one maintains success at a careful distance from family recognition. These childhood roles—the achiever, the rebel, the peacekeeper—often reflect attachment adaptations that persist into adulthood.

Emotional availability: One sibling might crave deeper connection, regularly starting heart-to-heart conversations, while another maintains surface-level engagement. The anxious sister sends long, emotional texts about wanting a closer connection; the avoidant brother responds with brief, practical updates. Their different comfort levels with intimacy create a push-pull that mirrors their early attachment experiences.

Conflict patterns: Watch how siblings handle disagreements: The anxiously attached might rush to repair even minor conflicts, fearing relationship damage. In contrast, avoidant siblings might withdraw completely until things "blow over." Secure siblings address issues directly, maintaining connection even during difficulty.

Crisis response: Major life events most clearly reveal attachment patterns. When parents age, or family challenges arise, siblings often fall into familiar roles: the over-functioning anxious sibling who takes charge of everything, the avoidant one who helps practically but stays emotionally distant, and the secure one who balances involvement with boundaries.

Extended Family Dynamics

Talk to different people, and you'll hear various stories about what happens around the table during Christmas, Thanksgiving, or other major family gatherings. There's the aunt who pulls you aside to critique everyone else's parenting, the uncle who keeps his emotional distance with jokes and surface-level conversation, and the grand-parent who constantly needs reassurance that you're eating enough, calling enough, and living up to their standards.

These dynamics aren't random personality quirks, but attachment patterns across generations. Extended family relationships often carry the weight of unspoken expectations, inherited trauma, and complex loyalties. The same aunt criticizing everyone's parenting might act from her anxious attachment, while the distant uncle's avoidance might stem from years of family emotional patterns.

These gatherings become stages where everyone's attachment style performs its familiar role: the anxiously attached relatives who try to control every detail to ensure connection, the avoidant ones who find reasons to arrive late and leave early, the secure ones who navigate the emotional currents with steady presence. Each interaction reveals individual patterns and the larger story of how families teach and transmit attachment across time.

Now let's look at some of the other ways through which these dynamics show up in interactions:

Holiday Gatherings: Watch how attachment styles play out around the family table. Anxious relatives fuss over every detail and seek constant connection, while avoidant ones limit their time and maintain emotional distance. In contrast, secure family members move quickly between engagement and space. These aren't random behaviors, but deeply ingrained patterns of relating.

Multigenerational patterns: Grandparents often show us where family attachment patterns began. For example, a grandmother's need to control every holiday detail might explain her daughter's anxiety around family gatherings, and a grandfather's difficulty expressing emotion might illuminate why his children struggle with emotional intimacy. These patterns pass down until someone decides to change them.

Cultural expectations: Family culture adds another layer to attachment dynamics. Some families expect constant connection and involvement, while others value independence. These expectations can either heal or heighten attachment wounds, especially when family members have different needs for closeness.

Boundary testing: Extended family presents unique challenges for maintaining healthy boundaries. From the aunt who expects immediate responses to all her messages to the cousin who freely shares private information, each relationship requires clear but kind limits that respect both connection and personal space.

We can't choose our family, and we can't control how we let them participate in our lives, but we can choose how we respond to the dynamics they bring. Understanding attachment patterns helps transform judgment into compassion—seeing the anxious aunt's frequent calls as attempts at connection rather than intrusion and recognizing the distant uncle's silence as learned protection rather than rejection.

We can honor our family bonds while protecting our peace, maintain a connection while setting boundaries, and carry forward healthy traditions while leaving behind the patterns that no longer serve.

Friendship and Loyalty

They say that friends are the family we choose, but our attachment patterns often choose for us before we realize it. Think about your closest friends—the one who never fails to text back within minutes or the one who disappears for weeks and then resurfaces as if no time has passed. These aren't just personality differences, but attachment styles playing out in friendship.

Our earliest experiences of connection write the script for how we show up in friendships. The anxiously attached friend might intensify new connections, while the avoidant maintains careful distance through busyness. The securely attached friend navigates closeness and independence with natural ease, creating space for both deep connection and comfortable silence.

These patterns reveal themselves most clearly in handling inevitable friendship challenges—when someone needs support, schedules get busy, or misunderstandings arise. Each response echoes our earliest lessons about love, trust, and loyalty. Understanding these patterns helps transform friendship from unconscious reaction to conscious choice, creating space for deeper, more authentic connections.

The Key Elements of Friendship

Trust and Loyalty in Friendships

Trust in friendships mirrors our attachment patterns. Anxious friends might test loyalty through constant availability checks or need frequent reassurance. Avoidant friends show trust through respect for independence, sometimes mistaken for lack of care. Secure friends balance intimacy with autonomy, creating space where trust grows naturally through consistency and understanding.

Navigating Conflict in Friendships

Sarah and Maya's decade-long friendship hit turbulence over a misinterpreted Instagram post. While Maya crafted careful texts explaining her hurt feelings for three days, Sarah muted notifications and dove into work projects. Their different responses to this minor conflict revealed deeper attachment patterns at play—Maya's anxious need to repair connections immediately clashed with Sarah's avoidant tendency to create distance until emotions calm.

Conflict reveals our attachment blueprints with striking clarity. Watch how friendship tensions unfold: an unreturned call sparks a spiral of worried messages from one friend while another responds with increased distance. One friend must process feelings immediately through long conversations, while another requires solitude to sort through emotions.

These patterns shape both the intensity and duration of friendship conflicts:

- Anxious friends might amplify minor misunderstandings into relationship threats.

- Avoidant friends might minimize significant issues to avoid emotional confrontation.

- Secure friends maintain perspective while addressing genuine concerns.

- Mixed attachment styles often create cycles of pursuit and withdrawal.

The path through friendship conflict requires understanding both your patterns and your friends. Sometimes, this means learning to accommodate an avoidant friend's need for space or helping an anxious friend feel secure without sacrificing your boundaries. True friendship grows stronger not from avoiding conflict but from learning to navigate it while keeping the connection intact.

Support Systems and Friendships

Support systems reveal not just what we give, but how we give it. For instance, during Elena's mother's illness, she received two distinct types of support. First, Rachel showed up with schedules, meal plans, and organized care rotas, while Sofia called daily to listen and hold space for tears. Both cared deeply, but their attachment styles colored how they expressed it.

How We Offer Support:

Anxiously attached: Friends become hyper-attuned to others' needs and often anticipate them before they're expressed. Their support stems from a deep need to prove their worth through caring for others. Still, while their dedication runs deep, they frequently exhaust themselves by offering help beyond their capacity, staying on the phone for hours despite fatigue, or dropping everything to be there for friends even when it disrupts their well-being.

Avoidant support style: Friends with avoidant attachment offer support through practical actions instead of emotional presence. They excel at researching solutions and creating action plans during crises. When friends face challenges, avoidant supporters focus on tangible help—organizing resources, solving logistical problems, and offering concrete solutions. This style of support provides reliable help while maintaining emotional distance.

Secure support: B-attached friends provide support with a natural equilibrium between practical help and emotional presence. They maintain clear boundaries while remaining reliably available. Their grounded sense of self allows them to offer meaningful support without becoming overwhelmed or distant. This balanced approach creates space for both giving and receiving care sustainably.

Mixed attachment dynamics: Support becomes more complex when different attachment styles interact in friendship. For example, an anxious friend's intensive care might overwhelm an avoidant receiver, while an avoidant's practical approach might feel emotionally insufficient to a worried friend. Understanding these differences helps friends appreciate various forms of support rather than expect everyone to care the same way.

Life's big moments—promotions, breakups, losses, celebrations—highlight these patterns. Notice how different friends respond:

- Some are overwhelmed with constant check-ins and help.

- Others maintain distance while sending practical resources.

- A few manage to provide space while staying reliably present.

- Many navigate between these styles depending on their capacity.

The healthiest support systems blend different strengths: the anxious friend who never forgets important dates, the avoidant friend who excels in crisis logistics, and the secure friend who knows when to step in and back.

Understanding these patterns helps create friendship networks in which everyone can give and receive support authentically rather than depleting.

Learning to recognize and respect these differences alters how we view friendship support. It's not about changing how friends show up but appreciating the unique ways each person expresses care while communicating our own needs.

You can be a good friend while honoring your attachment style. The key is to understand how you naturally give and receive care. The intensity of the anxious friend brings depth to relationships, the practicality of the avoidant offers steady ground during the chaos, and the balance of the secure friend helps everyone find their footing. These aren't flaws to fix but patterns to understand and work with intentionally.

True friendship grows from this understanding, from creating space for different ways of showing up. When we recognize that our avoidant friend's practical support carries as much care as our anxious friend's emotional presence, we build relationships that honor connection and authenticity. Each style brings its gifts to friendship, enriching our support systems through their unique expressions of love.

Attachment in Different Life Stages

Our attachment needs and expressions evolve throughout life, influenced by developmental changes, life transitions, and accumulated relationship experiences. Understanding how attachment manifests across different life stages helps us adapt our approach to relationships and recognize that growth and change are always possible.

Young Adulthood (18-30):

- Exploring identity through romantic relationships.

- Learning to balance independence with connection.

- Often repeating familiar attachment patterns from childhood.

- Prime time for developing earned security through new relationships.

Midlife (30-50):

- Attachment patterns often stabilize but remain changeable.

- Parenting may trigger our own attachment experiences.

- Career relationships become increasingly important.

- Opportunity for deep healing through conscious relationship work.

Later Life (50+):

- Attachment security often increases with life experience.

- Focus shifts to legacy relationships and generational healing.

- Grand parenting offers new opportunities for secure attachment.

- Facing loss and mortality can deepen appreciation for connection.

Understanding that attachment is a lifelong journey helps normalize the ongoing work of relationship growth and encourages hope for positive change at any stage of life.

This comprehensive view of attachment across relationship types reveals that our earliest patterns of connection truly are the blueprint for all human relationships. By understanding these patterns, we gain the power to choose more conscious, secure ways of relating in every area of our lives—from our intimate partnerships to our digital interactions, from our family dynamics to our professional relationships.

The goal isn't to eliminate our attachment style but to understand it so thoroughly that we can work with it rather than being controlled by it. In this understanding lies the key to creating more fulfilling, authentic connections across all the relationships that matter in our lives.

Chapter Ten

Personal Growth and Empowerment

"I used to think healing meant fixing myself," reflects Maria during her last therapy session. I now understand that I must work with, rather than against, my attachment patterns.

Personal growth in attachment work isn't about becoming a different person—it's about becoming more fully yourself while expanding your capacity for secure connection (Tatkin, 2012). This journey, **which** requires patience, self-compassion, and realistic expectations about change, is not a race but a steady, reassuring walk towards a more secure self.

Understanding the Growth Process

The Spiral Nature of Healing

Attachment healing rarely follows a linear path. Instead, it resembles a spiral staircase—you may revisit familiar emotional territory but from a slightly fresh vantage point each time (Herman, 2015).

What to expect:

- **Setbacks are normal:** Old patterns will resurface, especially during stress.

- **Progress isn't always visible:** Internal changes often precede external shifts.

- **Growth happens in layers:** Each experience of healing prepares you for deeper work.

- **Integration takes time:** New patterns need practice to become natural.

Example: After six months of therapy, James thought he'd "conquered" his avoidant patterns. When his relationship hit a rough patch, he found himself withdrawing again. Instead of seeing this as a failure, his therapist helped him recognize this as information—his nervous system was still learning to stay connected during conflicts.

Earned Security: The Goal of Growth Work

"Earned security" refers to individuals who develop secure attachment patterns later in life, despite having experienced insecurity in their early years (Main & Goldwyn, 1998). This isn't about erasing your history but integrating it in ways that support rather than hinder connection.

Characteristics of earned security:

- Awareness of your attachment patterns without being controlled by them.

- Ability to regulate emotions while staying connected to others.

- Capacity to repair relationship ruptures effectively.

- Integration of your attachment style's strengths while managing its challenges.

- Resilience during relationship stress without losing perspective.

Building Internal Security

Developing Self-Compassion

Self-compassion forms the foundation of all healing work (Neff, 2021). It involves treating yourself with the same kindness you'd offer a struggling friend.

The three components of self-compassion:

Self-kindness vs. self-judgment: Instead of: "I'm being anxious and clingy again. I'm such a mess."Try: "I'm feeling scared about this relationship. That makes sense, given my history. How can I care for myself right now?"

Common humanity vs. isolation: Instead of: "I'm the only one who struggles with this. Something's wrong with me."Try: "Many people struggle with relationship anxiety. I'm not alone in this experience."

Mindfulness vs. over-identification: Instead of: "I AM anxious. This is who I am."Try: "I'm FEELING anxious right now. This is a temporary state, not my identity."

Daily self-compassion practices:

- **Morning intention:** "How can I treat myself with kindness today?"

- **Midday check-in:** "What do I need right now to feel supported?"

- **Evening reflection:** "How did I show myself compassion today?"

- **Difficult moments:** Place hand on heart, take deep breaths, offer yourself words of comfort

Building Emotional Regulation Skills

Emotional regulation doesn't mean eliminating difficult emotions but learning to be with them without being overwhelmed (Siegel, 2020).

The window of tolerance concept: Everyone has a "window" where they can handle emotions and stress effectively. Trauma and insecure attachment often narrow this window. Healing work gradually expands it.

Signs you're outside your window:

- **Hyperarousal:** Racing heart, rapid breathing, overwhelming anxiety, racing thoughts.

- **Hypoarousal:** Numbness, disconnection, difficulty accessing emotions, mental fog.

Expanding your window of tolerance:

Mindfulness practices:

- **Body scan meditation:** 10 minutes daily, noticing sensations without changing them.

- **Breath awareness:** Following natural breath rhythm without forcing changes.

- **Emotion labeling:** "I notice anger arising," "I'm feeling sadness in my chest"

Somatic practices:

- **Progressive muscle relaxation:** Tensing and releasing muscle groups systematically.

- **Grounding exercises:** Feeling feet on the floor, noticing five things you can see/hear/touch.

- **Movement:** Walking, stretching, dancing to release emotional energy.

Cognitive practices:

- **Thought observation:** Watching thoughts without immediately believing or acting on them.

- **Reality testing:** "What evidence supports this thought? What evidence contradicts it?"

- **Self-talk reframing:** Speaking to yourself as you would a good friend.

Creating Internal Safety

Internal safety means feeling secure within yourself regardless of external circumstances (van der Kolk, 2021).

Daily practices for internal safety:

Morning routine:

- Set intentions for how you want to show up in relationships.

- Practice affirmations that reinforce your worth: "I am worthy of love and respect".

- Visualize yourself handling challenging situations with grace.

Throughout the day:

- Check-in with your emotional state regularly: "How am I feeling right now?"

- Practice grounding when you notice anxiety or overwhelm.

- Use positive self-talk during difficult moments.

Evening routine:

- Reflect on moments you responded differently than your old patterns.

- Practice gratitude for your growth, however small.

- Release the day's difficulties through journaling or meditation.

Breaking Negative Patterns

Recognizing Your Triggers

Understanding what activates your attachment system allows conscious choice rather than automatic reaction (Levine & Heller, 2010).

Common attachment triggers:

- **Communication changes:** Delayed responses, different tone, less frequent contact.

- **Emotional unavailability:** Partner seems distant, preoccupied, or stressed.

- **Social situations:** Meeting new people, feeling excluded, comparing yourself to others.

- **Life transitions:** Job changes, moving, relationship milestones.

- **Conflict:** Disagreements, criticism, feeling misunderstood.

Trigger tracking exercise: For two weeks, notice and record:

1. **Situation:** What happened immediately before you felt triggered?

2. **Physical response:** How did your body react (heart rate, breathing, tension)?

3. **Emotional response:** What emotions arose (fear, anger, sadness, shame)?

4. **Thoughts:** What stories did your mind create about the situation?

5. **Behavior:** How did you respond? What did you do or not do?

6. **Outcome:** How did others respond? How did you feel afterward?

Pattern recognition: After two weeks, review your entries for patterns:

- Which situations consistently trigger you?

- What themes run through your emotional responses?

- How do your behaviors affect your relationships?

- Where do you see opportunities for different responses?

The PAUSE Practice

Between trigger and response lies the space where transformation happens. The PAUSE practice creates that crucial gap (Siegel, 2020):

Physical awareness: Notice body sensations without trying to change them.

Acknowledge emotions: Name what you're feeling without judgment.

Understand the trigger: Recognize what activated your attachment system.

Select response: Choose conscious action rather than automatic re-action.

Engage mindfully: Respond from a place of awareness rather than fear.

Example: When Sophia's boyfriend doesn't respond to her text for three hours, she notices her heart racing (Physical), acknowledges feeling afraid of abandonment (Acknowledge), recognizes this pattern from childhood (Understand), chooses to use self-soothing techniques instead of sending multiple texts (Select), and later expresses her needs directly (Engage).

Creating New Response Patterns

Start small: Begin practicing new responses in low-stakes situations before applying them to major triggers

Use implementation intentions:

- "When I feel [trigger], I will [specific action],"

- "When I feel anxious about my partner's silence, I will take five deep breaths and remind myself that silence doesn't equal rejection,"

- "When I feel overwhelmed by emotional conversations, I will ask for a 10-minute break to regulate before continuing,"

- "When I feel criticized, I will listen for any valid points rather than immediately defending,"

Practice the 24-hour rule: For important decisions or responses, wait 24 hours when possible to ensure you're responding from clarity rather than activation.

Build success gradually:

- Week 1: Notice triggers without changing responses.

- Week 2: Practice the PAUSE technique once daily.

- Week 3: Implement one new response per week.

- Week 4: Celebrate progress and identify the next growth area.

Developing Healthy Relationships

Choosing Growth-Supporting Relationships

Not all relationships support your journey toward security. Learning to identify and prioritize relationships that encourage growth is essential (Johnson, 2019).

Relationships that support security:

- **Consistency:** People who follow through on commitments and communicate reliably.

- **Emotional safety:** Individuals who respond to vulnerability with care rather than judgment.

- **Growth mindset:** Those who view challenges as opportunities rather than threats.

- **Mutual respect:** Relationships with balanced give-and-take where both people's needs matter.

- **Healthy boundaries:** People who respect your limits and maintain their own.

Relationships that hinder security:

- **Inconsistency:** People whose availability and affection are unpredictable.

- **Emotional Unsafety:** Those who respond to vulnerability with criticism, dismissal, or retaliation.

- **Drama addiction:** Individuals who create chaos or thrive on relationship turmoil.

- **One-sided dynamics:** Relationships where you consistently give more than you receive.

- **Boundary violations:** People who repeatedly disrespect your stated limits.

Building New Relationship Skills

Communication skills for secure relating:

"I" statements: Express feelings and needs without blame.

- Instead of: "You never listen to me,"

- Try: "I feel unheard when conversations shift away from my concerns,"

Validation before problem-solving:

- Instead of: "Here's what you should do about that problem,"

- Try: "That sounds really difficult. How are you feeling about it?"

Direct need expression:

- Instead of: Dropping hints or expecting others to read your mind

- Try: "I need some reassurance that we're okay after yesterday's disagreement,"

Repair attempts during conflict:

- "I can see we're both getting activated. Can we take a break and come back to this?"

- "I'm sorry I raised my voice. That wasn't helpful. Can we start over?"

- "Even though we disagree about this, I want you to know I care about you."

Boundary setting with care:

- "I love spending time with you, and I also need Sunday mornings to myself to recharge."

- "I want to support you through this difficulty, and I need to limit our phone calls to an hour so I can manage my stress."

Dating and Partner Selection Through an Attachment Lens

Green flags for secure partnership:

- **Emotional availability:** Can discuss feelings without shutting down or becoming overwhelmed.

- **Consistency:** Behavior matches words; reliability in both small and large commitments.

- **Growth orientation:** Interested in personal development and willing to work on relationship challenges.

- **Conflict skills:** Can disagree respectfully and work toward resolution.

- **Independence:** Has individual interests, friendships, and goals outside the relationship.

Red flags to watch for:

- **Love bombing:** Intense early attachment that feels overwhelming rather than genuinely loving.

- **Hot and cold patterns:** Inconsistent availability and affection that keep you guessing.

- **Boundary resistance:** Responds poorly when you express needs or limits.

- **Emotional unavailability:** Struggles to express feelings or connect during vulnerable moments.

- **Drama patterns:** Creates or attracts chaos, conflict, or crisis regularly.

Dating strategies for different attachment styles:

For anxious attachment:

- Practice tolerating uncertainty rather than seeking immediate relationship definition.

- Maintain individual friendships and interests during early dating.

- Pay attention to how potential partners respond to your emotional expressions.

- Look for consistency over intensity in early relationship stages.

For avoidant attachment:

- Challenge yourself to share something personal on each date rather than keeping conversations surface-level.

- Notice and communicate appreciation for your date's emotional expressions.

- Practice staying present during emotionally intimate moments rather than changing subjects.

- Look for partners who can respect your need for space while also encouraging connection.

For disorganized attachment:

- Consider dating a break while focusing on individual healing if patterns are chaotic.

- Work with a therapist to understand your relationship triggers before entering serious relationships.

- Look for partners who demonstrate emotional stability and

patience.

- Practice sharing your attachment needs directly rather than through behavior.

Professional Support and Therapy

When to Seek Professional Help

While many attachment patterns can improve through self-awareness and practice, professional support accelerates healing and provides safety for processing deeper wounds.

Consider therapy when:

- Relationship patterns consistently cause distress despite your efforts to change them.

- Trauma history impacts your ability to trust or connect with others.

- Emotional reactions feel overwhelming or disproportionate to situations.

- Self-harm, substance use, or other destructive coping mechanisms are present.

- You feel stuck in repetitive relationship cycles despite wanting to change.

Types of Therapy for Attachment Healing

Emotionally Focused Therapy (EFT):

- Specifically designed for attachment issues in couples and individuals.

- Focuses on accessing and expressing emotions safely.

- Helps identify negative relationship cycles and create new patterns.

- Research-proven effectiveness for attachment-related difficulties.

Internal Family Systems (IFS):

- Views the self as composed of different "parts" with various roles and functions.

- Helps heal wounded aspects of self while strengthening core Self-leadership.

- Particularly effective for trauma-related attachment issues.

- Promotes internal harmony and self-compassion.

Somatic therapies (SE, SP, NARM):

- Work with trauma and attachment patterns stored in the body.

- Help restore nervous system regulation and resilience.

- Include body awareness and movement in the healing

process.

- Effective for early trauma that may not be accessible through talk therapy alone.

EMDR (Eye Movement Desensitization and Reprocessing):

- Processes traumatic memories that fuel attachment fears.

- Reduces emotional charge of past experiences.

- It helps integrate difficult experiences in healthier ways.

- Particularly effective for specific traumatic events.

Dialectical Behavior Therapy (DBT):

- Teaches practical skills for emotional regulation and distress tolerance.

- Includes interpersonal effectiveness and mindfulness training.

- It is particularly helpful for disorganized attachment patterns.

- Provides concrete tools for managing intense emotions.

Finding the Right Therapist

Questions to ask potential therapists:

- Do you have specific training in attachment theory and trauma?

- What approaches do you use for attachment-related difficulties?

- How do you handle your attachment style in therapeutic relationships?

- What does the healing process typically look like in your practice?

- How do you know when clients are ready to end therapy?

Green flags in therapists:

- Warmth and genuineness combined with appropriate professional boundaries.

- Ability to attune to your emotional states without becoming overwhelmed.

- Consistency in scheduling, communication, and therapeutic approach.

- Willingness to discuss the therapeutic relationship itself when needed.

- Cultural competence and sensitivity to your background and identity.

Building Support Networks

Creating Your Support Ecosystem

Healthy attachment healing requires community. No single person—not even a therapist—can meet all your attachment needs.

Types of support to cultivate:

Emotional support: People who listen without trying to fix, validate your feelings, and offer comfort during difficult times.

Practical support: Individuals who help with concrete needs—rides to appointments, meal prep during illness, childcare assistance.

Social support: Friends who share interests and provide fun, connection, and belonging.

Spiritual support: A community that shares your values and provides meaning, whether religious, philosophical, or nature-based.

Professional support: Therapists, coaches, mentors, or other professionals who guide your growth.

Example support network:

- **Best friend:** Emotional support and fun social connection.

- **Family member:** Practical support and shared history.

- **Therapist:** Professional guidance and trauma healing.

- **Support group:** Shared experience with attachment healing.

- **Spiritual community:** Meaning-making and values alignment.

- **Romantic partner:** Intimate emotional and physical connection.

- **Work mentor:** Professional growth and career support.

Support Groups and Community Healing

Benefits of group support:

- Reduces isolation and shame around attachment struggles.

- Provides modeling of healthy relationship skills.

- Offers the opportunity to practice new patterns in a safe environment.

- Creates accountability and encouragement for growth work.

Types of groups to consider:

- **Attachment-focused therapy groups:** Led by trained professionals.

- **Codependents Anonymous (CoDA):** For unhealthy relationship patterns.

- **Adult Children of Alcoholics (ACA):** For family-of-origin trauma.

- **Support groups for specific trauma types:** Sexual abuse, domestic violence, childhood neglect.

- **Online communities:** Forums and virtual groups for attachment healing.

Integrating Growth into Daily Life

Creating Daily Practices

Consistency in small practices creates more lasting change than sporadic intense efforts.

Morning practices (5-10 minutes):

- Set intention for how you want to show up in relationships today.

- Practice gratitude for your support system.

- Visualize handling potential triggers with your new tools.

- Affirm your worth and commitment to growth.

Midday check-ins (2-3 minutes):

- Notice your emotional state without judgment.

- Use grounding techniques if feeling activated.

- Practice self-compassion if you've reverted to old patterns.

- Appreciate any moments you've responded differently.

Evening practices (10-15 minutes):

- Journal about relationship interactions and what you learned.

- Reflect on progress made, however small.

- Release the day's difficulties through meditation or breathwork.

- Set intentions for tomorrow's growth opportunities.

Measuring Progress

Attachment healing progress isn't always obvious. Look for these subtle shifts:

Internal changes:

- Less time spent in emotional overwhelm.

- Increased ability to self-soothe during distress.

- Greater awareness of triggers before they control behavior.

- More self-compassion during difficult moments.

Relational changes:

- Conflicts that resolve more quickly and thoroughly.

- Increased comfort with both intimacy and independence.

- Better ability to express needs directly.

- More satisfying and stable relationships over time.

Behavioral changes:

- Different choices during triggering situations.

- Less reactive responses to others' attachment behaviors.

- Increased willingness to be vulnerable when appropriate.

- Better boundary setting without guilt or anger.

Preventing Relapse and Maintaining Growth

Understanding Setbacks

Setbacks aren't failures—they're information about what still needs attention and opportunities to practice recovery skills.

Common setback triggers:

- Major life transitions (job loss, moving, relationship changes).

- Health crises or family emergencies.

- Anniversary dates of traumatic events.

- Relationship milestones that activate attachment fears.

- High stress periods that overwhelm coping resources.

Healthy setback response:

1. **Normalize the experience:** "This is part of the healing process."

2. **Use your tools:** Return to practices that have helped before.

3. **Seek support:** Reach out to your network rather than isolating.

4. **Practice self-compassion:** Treat yourself with kindness

rather than criticism.

5. **Learn from the experience:** What can this setback teach you about your ongoing needs?

Maintenance Strategies

Continue therapy periodically: "Booster" sessions during transitions or stressful periods.

Maintain support connections: Regular contact with people who support your growth.

Keep practicing daily tools: Don't abandon practices once you feel better.

Monitor stress levels: Recognize when you need extra support before reaching a crisis.

Celebrate progress: Acknowledge how far you've come, especially during difficult periods.

The Lifelong Journey

Attachment healing isn't a destination but a lifelong practice of growing more secure in your relationships with yourself and others. Each challenge becomes an opportunity to practice new patterns, each relationship a chance to heal old wounds.

Your attachment style represents both your greatest vulnerability and your unique gift. Anxious attachment brings a deep capacity for love and emotional attunement. Avoidant attachment offers stability and independence. Disorganized attachment often includes creativity and resilience. Secure attachment provides balance and flexibility.

The goal isn't to eliminate your attachment style but to work with it consciously—honoring its gifts while addressing its limitations, and using its strengths while healing its wounds.

As you continue this journey, remember:

- Growth happens in spirals, not straight lines

- Small daily practices create lasting change

- Setbacks are part of the process, not signs of failure

- You're capable of forming the secure, loving relationships you desire

- Your healing contributes to breaking generational patterns and creating a more secure world

The work you're doing to understand and heal your attachment patterns doesn't just benefit you—it ripples out to every relationship you touch, creating more security, love, and connection in the world.

Personal growth provides the foundation for secure relationships, but understanding the broader applications of attachment theory helps us recognize how these patterns show up in every area of life. Let's explore how to apply these insights across all your relationships and life contexts.

Moving Forward

E lena puts down her journal and looks out the window at the morning light filtering through her apartment. Six months ago, she would have been checking her phone obsessively, analyzing her boyfriend's last text for hidden meanings, creating stories about his silence. Today, she notices the urge to check her phone, acknowledges the familiar flutter of anxiety, and chooses instead to finish her coffee and get ready for work.

"The anxiety is still there," she reflects, "but it doesn't run my life anymore."

This is what attachment healing looks like—not the elimination of all relationship challenges, but the development of choice in how you respond to them. It's the difference between being controlled by your patterns and working with them consciously.

Effective communication in attachment-aware relationships isn't about eliminating differences in communication styles but about developing fluency in each other's attachment languages. The anxious partner's emotional intensity and the avoidant partner's practical processing both have value when understood and appreciated rather than criticized or changed.

The goal isn't perfect communication but secure communication—interactions that leave both partners feeling heard, valued, and emotionally safe. This requires understanding that your partner's communication style developed for good reasons and serves important functions, even when it differs dramatically from your own.

Building these skills takes time, patience, and often professional support. Communication patterns developed over decades don't change overnight. But with consistent practice and mutual commitment to growth, couples can develop communication cultures that honor their attachment differences while building the security and connection they both desire.

Anxious partners can learn to express needs without overwhelming urgency. The avoidant partner can learn to share emotions without feeling engulfed. And, the disorganized partner can learn to communicate complexity without chaos. And all partners can learn to create the emotional safety that allows to flourish regardless of their attachment starting points.

By being patient and intentional in the work, you will find the promise of relationships where both partners feel truly known and deeply loved. This is not despite their attachment styles but through the conscious, skillful understanding of them and their origins.

The Transformation Is Subtle but Profound

Attachment healing rarely announces itself with dramatic revelations or sudden personality changes. Instead, it whispers through small moments:

- Staying present for one extra minute during a hard conversation

- Asking for what you need instead of hoping others will guess

- Sitting with uncertainty without immediately creating stories

- Offering comfort to yourself during distress instead of seeking it frantically from others

- Recognizing your triggers without being overwhelmed by them

These seemingly small shifts accumulate over time, creating relationships that feel different—safer, more authentic, more sustainable.

What You've Learned

Through reading this book, you've discovered that:

Attachment styles are adaptations, not disorders. Every pattern developed as an intelligent response to early experiences. Anxious sensitivity once protected you from abandonment. Avoidant independence once shielded you from disappointment. Your disorganized complexity reflects your early attempts to navigate impossible circumstances.

Understanding creates choice. Awareness of your patterns interrupts their automatic activation. The space between trigger and response becomes a place of possibility rather than inevitability.

Healing happens in relationship. While individual work provides an essential foundation, attachment wounds heal through corrective relationship experiences—with therapists, friends, partners, or community members who offer consistency, safety, and genuine care.

Security is possible at any age. Regardless of your early experiences, you can develop "earned security"—the ability to form healthy relationships through conscious awareness and practice.

Your attachment style is both gift and challenge. Each style brings unique strengths to relationships alongside its limitations. Growth means amplifying the gifts while addressing the challenges.

The Ongoing Journey

Attachment healing isn't a destination, but a lifelong practice. You'll continue to encounter situations that trigger old patterns, relationships that challenge your growth, and life circumstances that test your new skills. This isn't failure—it's the human experience.

What changes isn't the absence of challenges, but your relationship with them. Where you once felt controlled by your patterns, you now have tools. You no longer have to feel isolated in your struggles. You now have understanding and support. Where you once believed your relationship difficulties were inevitable, you now know change is possible.

Your Ripple Effect

The work you've done to understand and heal your attachment patterns extends far beyond your personal relationships. Every interaction becomes an opportunity to model secure relating:

- **In your family:** Breaking generational patterns of insecure attachment

- **With your children:** Providing the emotional safety and attunement that promotes secure attachment

- **In your friendships:** Creating relationships based on authenticity rather than performance

- **At work:** Contributing to psychologically safe, collaborative environments

- **In your community:** Extending empathy and understanding to others' attachment struggles

Your healing contributes to a more secure world, one relationship at a time.

Practical Tools for Continued Growth

Daily practices to maintain your growth:

Morning intention setting: "How do I want to show up in my relationships today?"

Midday check-ins: "What am I feeling right now? What do I need?"

Evening reflection: "Where did I respond differently today? What can I learn from my interactions?"

Weekly relationship review: "How are my relationships feeling? Where do I want to focus my attention?"

Monthly growth assessment: "What patterns am I noticing? What support do I need?"

When challenges arise:

1. **Pause and breathe:** Create space between trigger and response

2. **Name what's happening:** "I'm feeling activated by my

partner's distance"

3. **Use your tools:** Self-soothing, grounding, reaching out for support

4. **Choose consciously:** Respond from awareness rather than automatic reaction

5. **Practice self-compassion:** Honor your humanity in the learning process

Building Your Support Network

Continue cultivating relationships that support your growth:

Professional support: Therapists, coaches, or counselors who understand attachment work

Peer support: Support groups, online communities, or friends on similar growth journeys

Intimate relationships: Partners, close friends, or family members who encourage your authenticity

Community connections: Groups that share your values and provide belonging

Spiritual or philosophical support: Communities or practices that provide meaning and perspective

Signs You're Growing

Watch for these indicators of increasing security:

Internal shifts:

- Less time spent in emotional overwhelm

- Increased self-compassion during difficulties

- Greater awareness of your patterns without being controlled by them

- More consistent sense of self-worth

Relational changes:

- Conflicts that resolve more quickly and completely

- Increased comfort with both intimacy and independence

- Better ability to express needs and maintain boundaries

- More satisfying relationships overall

Life changes:

- Decisions made from values rather than fears

- Increased resilience during stress or transitions

- Greater capacity for joy and pleasure

- Sense of purpose that extends beyond personal relationships

When Setbacks Happen

They will happen. Growth isn't linear, and setbacks are part of the healing process. When old patterns resurface:

Remember: This is information, not failure. Your nervous system is simply doing what it learned to do for protection.

Practice self-compassion: Treat yourself with the same kindness you'd offer a struggling friend.

Return to your tools: Use the practices that have helped you before.

Seek support: Reach out to your network rather than isolating.

Learn from the experience: What triggered the setback? What additional support or skills might help?

Celebrate your awareness: that you recognize the pattern shows how much you've grown.

Your Unique Path

There's no "right" way to heal attachment wounds. Your journey will be shaped by:

- Your specific attachment history and current circumstances

- Your cultural background and family dynamics

- Your available resources and support systems

- Your personality, interests, and natural strengths

- The timing and readiness of your healing process

Honor your individual path while learning from others' experiences. What works for someone else may not work for you, and that's perfectly normal.

The Invitation

This book ends, but your attachment growth continues. You're invited to:

Keep learning: Read additional resources, attend workshops, explore new therapeutic approaches

Stay connected: Maintain relationships that support your growth and seek new ones that challenge you to continue growing

Practice compassion: Extend understanding to yourself and others as you all navigate the complexity of human relationships

Share your journey: Your story of healing can inspire and support others on their own paths

Trust the process: healing happens in its own timing, often in ways you don't expect

A Final Reflection

Your attachment style tells the story of your early adaptation to love and relationships. It reflects your intelligence, creativity, and resilience in the face of whatever circumstances shaped your early years. It's neither your fault nor your failure—it's your starting point.

From this foundation, you can build relationships that feel safe, authentic, and nourishing. You can love deeply without losing yourself, connect intimately without sacrificing your autonomy, and weather relationship storms without losing faith in the possibility of lasting connection.

The anxious heart can learn to love without fear. An avoidant spirit can discover that intimacy enhances rather than threatens independence. The disorganized soul can integrate its complexity into wholeness. Secure foundations can deepen and expand throughout life.

Your relationships—with yourself and others—are your greatest opportunities for healing, growth, and joy. Each interaction is a chance to practice new patterns, each conflict an opportunity for deeper understanding, each moment of connection a celebration of your capacity for love.

The work you've done to understand your attachment patterns isn't just personal development—it's a contribution to the healing of the world. Every secure relationship you create, every generational pattern you break, every moment of compassion you extend creates ripples that spread far beyond what you can see.

Your attachment journey continues. May it be filled with growth, connection, and the deep satisfaction that comes from relationships built on understanding, authenticity, and love.

The heart that has learned to love securely is a gift to the world.

"Being deeply loved by someone gives you strength, while loving someone deeply gives you courage." - Lao Tzu

Your journey toward secure attachment cultivates both—the strength that comes from experiencing safe love and the courage required to love openly despite past wounds. This is your invitation to continue growing, connecting, and contributing to a more securely attached world.

Self-Regulation Toolkit

Self-Regulation for Attachment Healing

A ttachment patterns influence how we react to closeness, conflict, and vulnerability—often in ways we don't consciously choose. Whether we cling tightly, pull away, or swing between both extremes, these reactions reflect our nervous system's learned adaptations to early relational experiences. Self-regulation isn't about suppressing emotion or "fixing" ourselves—it's about learning how to stay grounded and present, even when our old wiring screams otherwise.

This section offers self-regulation practices to support emotional balance and relational growth, especially for those with **anxious, avoidant, or disorganized attachment styles**. These tools teach us to calm our physiological responses, reflect before reacting, and connect with others in more stable, satisfying ways. Each practice is designed to meet the nervous system where it is and gently expand its capacity for safety, connection, and resilience.

1. Physical Regulation: Calming the Nervous System

Box Breathing

This four-part breathing technique helps restore calm by engaging the parasympathetic nervous system:

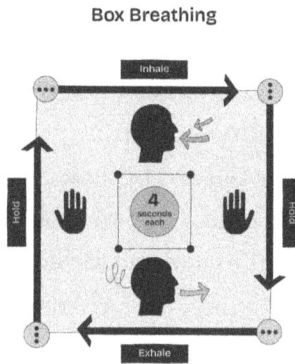

Box Breathing

- Inhale for 4 seconds

- Hold for 4 seconds

- Exhale for 4 seconds

- Hold for 4 seconds

Repeat for 1–3 minutes. This is especially helpful for anxious or disorganized individuals experiencing spiraling thoughts or panic.

Cold Water or Ice Stimulation

Splashing cold water on your face or holding an ice cube activates the "diving reflex," slowing the heart rate and calming physiological arousal. This is a quick reset when emotions feel overwhelming or when dissociation occurs.

Progressive Muscle Relaxation

Start at your feet and work up the body, tensing each muscle group for 5 seconds and then releasing. This grounds you in your body and helps counteract emotional overwhelm, especially useful for avoidant individuals who've become emotionally shut down.

Gentle Movement

Walking, stretching, or swaying helps discharge built-up tension and re-engage your body in the present moment. Movement can shift the nervous system from freezing or panic back to regulation.

2. Cognitive & Emotional Awareness: Naming the Experience

Label the Emotion

Say to yourself: *"This is attachment anxiety"* or *"My system is afraid of closeness."* Naming the emotional state activates your prefrontal cortex and reduces the intensity of the emotion.

Time-Box Worry

Give yourself 15 minutes to fully feel and process worries. Write everything down. When the timer ends, shift activities. This trains your brain to contain anxiety instead of letting it hijack your day—ideal for anxious and disorganized styles.

The 5-Minute Rule

Before sending a reassurance-seeking message or emotionally withdrawing, wait five minutes. During that time:

- Notice body sensations

- Identify what triggered your urge

- Ask: *"What do I truly need?"*
  This builds the muscle of intentional responding instead of reactive coping.

3. Self-Compassion and Soothing Inner Dialogues

Reframe Thought Patterns

When the mind jumps to worst-case scenarios ("They're pulling away," "I'll be abandoned"), try countering with grounded truths:

- "I don't have all the information yet."

- "This is a familiar fear, not necessarily reality."
  This helps anxious and disorganized individuals disrupt catastrophic thinking loops.

Self-Compassion Statements

Practice saying:

- "It's okay to feel this."

- "I learned this way of coping for a reason."

- "This doesn't make me broken—it makes me human." This builds internal safety and softens shame around attachment triggers.

4. Communication as Regulation

Direct Expression of Needs

Avoid hinting or withdrawing. Say:

- "I feel anxious when we go too long without checking in."

- "I need some space to process, and I'll reconnect soon."

For anxious styles, this builds clarity and reduces overthinking. For avoidant styles, it helps make internal boundaries visible rather than implied.

Check-In Rituals

Weekly check-ins (10–15 minutes) with a partner or close friend build connection through consistency. Use a simple format:

- "One thing I appreciated this week..."

- "One challenge I faced…"

- "One thing I need moving forward…"

This regularity helps disorganized styles feel safe in connection and builds predictability for avoidants.

5. Co-Regulation and Relational Safety

Mirroring or Matched Breathing

Sit back-to-back or side-by-side with a trusted person and breathe together. Matching pace calms the nervous system and builds synchrony, especially effective for disorganized individuals learning safe connection.

Shared Stillness or Activity

You don't always need conversation to connect. Try quiet companionship: cooking together, walking in silence, or sitting nearby with separate books. For avoidants, this respects their need for space while still fostering a relational presence.

You Got This

Self-regulation is the foundation of healing insecure attachment—not to eliminate the need for others, but to build the inner scaffolding that makes for a secure connection possible. With time, these practices can soften reactivity, expand emotional capacity, and make room for love that feels safe, mutual, and sustaining.

References

Journal Articles

Bartholomew, K., & Horowitz, L. M. (1991). Attachment styles among young adults: A test of a four-category model. *Journal of Personality and Social Psychology, 61*(2), 226–244. https://doi.or g/10.1037/0022-3514.61.2.226

Waters, T. E. A., & Roisman, G. I. (2021). The secure base script: A novel tool for understanding the nature and function of attachment representations across the lifespan. *Attachment & Human Development, 23*(2), 103-121. https://doi.org/10.1080/14616734.2020.18 37092

Books

Bowlby, J. (2021). *Attachment and loss: Volume I*. Basic Books. (Original work published 1969)

Brennan, K. A., Clark, C. L., & Shaver, P. R. (1998). Self-report measurement of adult romantic attachment: An integrative overview. In J. A. Simpson & W. S. Rholes (Eds.), *Attachment theory and close relationships* (pp. 46–76). Guilford Press.

Holmes, J., & Slade, A. (2022). *Attachment in therapeutic practice*. Sage Publications.

Levine, A., & Heller, R. (2010). *Attached: The new science of adult attachment and how it can help you find—and keep—love*. Tarcher-Perigee.

Mikulincer, M., & Shaver, P. R. (2023). *Attachment theory and close relationships: Theoretical foundations and new developments*. Guilford Press.

Schore, A. N. (2021). *The development of the unconscious mind*. W. W. Norton & Company.

Siegel, D. J. (2023). *Interpersonal neurobiology and the healing power of connection*. Norton Professional Books.

Sroufe, L. A., & Raby, K. L. (2021). *The development of the person: The Minnesota study of risk and adaptation from birth to adulthood*. Guilford Press.

van der Kolk, B. (2021). *The body keeps the score workbook*. Penguin Random House.

Government/Institutional Sources

National Collaborating Centre for Mental Health (UK). (2015, November). Introduction to children's attachment. In *National Institute for Health and Care Excellence (UK)*. https://www.ncbi.nlm.nih.gov/books/NBK356196/

Web Sources

Attachment style quiz: Free & fast attachment style test. (2022, November 18). *Attachment Project*. https://www.attachmentproject.com/attachment-style-quiz/

Braman, L. (2019, November 3). Understanding adult attachment styles: Illustrated guide. *LindsayBraman.com*. https://lindsaybram an.com/attachment-style-spectrum/

Cafasso, J. (2019, November 14). What is anxious attachment? *Healthline*. https://www.healthline.com/health/mental-health/an xious-attachment

Cherry, K. (2023). The different types of attachment styles. *Verywell Mind*. https://www.verywellmind.com/attachment-styles-2795344

Divecha, D. (2017, April 3). What is a secure attachment and why doesn't "attachment parenting" get you there? *Developmental S c i e n c e* . https://www.developmentalscience.com/blog/2017/3/31/what-is -a-secure-attachmentand-why-doesnt-attachment-parenting-get-yo u-there

Drescher, A. (2024, March 11). Disorganized attachment style: Traits and ways to cope. *Simply Psychology*. https://www.simplyps ychology.org/disorganized-attachment.html

Effa, C. (2022, December 6). How to fix an anxious attachment style. *Medical News Today*. https://www.medicalnewstoday.com/articles /how-to-fix-anxious-attachment-style

Franco, M. G. (2022, August 25). The trait that "super friends" have in common. *The At- lantic*. https://www.theatlantic.com/family/archive/2022/08/mak ing-keeping-friends-attachment-theory-styles/671222/

Friend problems? Maybe it's your attachment style. (2023, August 31). *Oprah Daily*. https://www.oprahdaily.com/life/relationships-l ove/a44903924/what-is-your-attachment-style/

Goldman, R. (2023, September 19). What is my attachment style? *Verywell Mind*. https://www.verywellmind.com/attachment-style-quiz-7562460

Ho, J. (n.d.). How to heal anxious attachment by prioritizing your own needs. *Greater Good*. https://greatergood.berkeley.edu/article/item/how_to_heal_anxious_attachment_by_prioritizing_your_own_needs

How to date someone with an avoidant attachment style. (2024, January 23). *Simply Psychology*. https://www.simplypsychology.org/dating-someone-with-an-avoidant-attachment.html

How to date someone with avoidant attachment style. (2023, December 8). *Attachment Project*. https://www.attachmentproject.com/avoidant-attachment-relationships/dating/

How your attachment style (and trauma) shows up in friendships. (2023, October 15). *The Healing Nest Blog*. https://thehealingnest.co.uk/blog/how-your-attachment-style-and-trauma-shows-up-in-friendships/

Kamau, B. (2023, January 12). How your attachment style impacts how you make friends. *Beatricekamau.com*. https://beatricekamau.com/2023/01/12/how-your-attachment-style-impacts-how-you-make-friends-182/

Lee, C. I. (2023, April 24). How attachment style shows up in friendships. *LA Concierge Psychologist*. https://laconciergepsychologist.com/blog/attachment-style-friendships/

Lewis, R. (2020, September 25). Types of attachment styles and what they mean. *Healthline*. https://www.healthline.com/health/parenting/types-of-attachment

Méndez, J. M. (2023, October 22). Navigating love: Strategies for dating an avoidant partner. *Medium*. https://medium.com/@janellemarinamendez/navigating-love -strategies-for-dating-an-avoidant-partner-934ed62ae724

Moore, L. (2023, June 28). What attachment styles teach us about our friendships. *ELLE*. https://www.elle.com/life-love/opinions-fe atures/a44285552/attachment-styles-in-friendships/

Schuster, S. (2023, July 30). How to tell if you have an anxious attachment style. *Health*. https://www.health.com/anxious-attach ment-style-7562046

Schwartz, A. (2014, July 2). Relationships change brain, heal attach-ment. *Arielle Schwartz, PhD*. https://drarielleschwartz.com/how-r elationships-change-brain-heal-attachment-dr-arielle-schwartz/

What is my attachment style? Take the quiz (+PDF). (2024, Septem-ber 16). *Simply Psychology*. https://www.simplypsychology.org/att achment-style-quiz.html

WFLA. (2023, October 6). Why you're close to some friends and not others: Attachment theory. *WFLA*. https://www.wfla.com/bloom-tampa-bay/bloom-relation ships/why-youre-close-to-some-friends-and-not-others-attachment-

www.ingramcontent.com/pod-product-compliance
Lightning Source LLC
Chambersburg PA
CBHW032054040426
42335CB00037B/708